ADDITIONAL PRAISE FOR *NATURAL LAW*

"This is a Guide that has considerable depth, indeed two distinct dimensions. The reader is first guided to the philosophical roots of natural law thinking in ancient and scholastic philosophy; then secondly to the Biblical evidence for natural law. The result makes for a first-rate, thought-provoking introduction."
— *Paul Helm, Professor Emeritus, King's College, London.*

"God's general revelation has not only a cosmic, but also a moral dimension. This much should be uncontroversial among Christian theologians and philosophers. During the twentieth century, however, it was widely held that the Reformation had done away with this moral side of general revelation which we call natural law. Happily, during the last decade that misreading has been successfully corrected, and we are now moving from retrieval to contemporary reflection. Fulford and Haines join this revival of Protestant consideration of natural law with a solid philosophical and biblical introduction. The authors and the Davenant Institute deserve our deepest thanks for making these issues accessible to a wide readership in such a clear and thoughtful book."
—*Manfred Svensson, Professor of Philosophy, University of the Andes, co-editor,* Aquinas Among the Protestants

D1627088

DAVENANT GUIDES seek to offer short and accessible introductions to key issues of current debate in theology and ethics, drawing on a magisterial Protestant perspective and defending its contemporary relevance today.

NATURAL LAW:

A Brief Introduction and Biblical Defense

BY DAVID HAINES AND ANDREW FULFORD

CONTENTS

INTRODUCTION

"IN THE BEGINNING, God created the heavens and the earth" (Gen. 1:1). "And God saw everything that he had made, and behold, it was very good" (Gen. 1:31). Christianity teaches that God created the universe out of nothing (*ex nihilo*). In accordance with the Jewish Scriptures, the teachings of Christ, and the witness of his Apostles, one of the foundational Christian declarations of faith, *the Nicene Creed*, begins, "We believe in one God the Father Almighty, Maker of heaven and earth, And of all things visible and invisible."[1] Furthermore, the *Westminster Confession of Faith*, one of the crucial creeds to be produced by Protestant theologians proclaims,

> It pleased God the Father, Son, and Holy Ghost, for the manifestation of the glory of his eternal power, wisdom, and goodness, in the beginning, to create or make of nothing the world, and all things therein, whether visi-

---

[1] Cf. Philip Schaff, *The History of Creeds*, vol. 1 of *The Creeds of Christendom*, ed. David S. Schaff, 6th ed. (1983; repr., Grand Rapids: Baker Books, 2007), 27.

ble or invisible, in the space of six days, and all very good.[2]

In the opening lines of the Bible and in the Church's creeds, we learn that God is the source of all creation, and that all created things were, in their divinely instituted natural states, *good*. As we will see, the very fact of divine creation seems to point towards what has been traditionally called *natural law*: the notion that there is, because of the divine intellect, a natural order within the created world by which each and every created being's goodness can be objectively judged, both on the level of being (ontological goodness), and, for human-beings specifically, on the level of human action (moral goodness). Ontological goodness is the foundation of moral goodness.

But, some might wonder, is not the doctrine of natural law an invention of Roman Catholic theologians—one both unbiblical and rejected by coherent Protestant theologians? It is true that natural law has not always been well received within Protestant ethics, and it seems to be less accepted today than ever. Whereas some Protestant works on Ethics do not even mention natural law,[3] other works, written by important Evangelical thinkers, seem to imply that the claim that unregenerate humans can discover what is good through some form of natural law departs from a truly Protestant theology. For Cornelius Van Til, the Roman Catholic approach to ethics is immediately disqualified from "either stating or defending a true Christian

---

2 "The Westminster Confession of Faith, 1647," in Philip Schaff, *The Evangelical Protestant Creeds*, vol. 3 of *The Creeds of Christendom*, 6th ed., ed. David S. Schaff (1983; repr., Grand Rapids: Baker Books, 2007), 611.

3 R. K. Harrison, ed., *The Encyclopedia of Biblical Ethics* (New York: Testament Books, 1992).

doctrine of human behavior," because the Catholic theologian

> admits that the natural man who makes himself the goal of his efforts, who uses his own experience instead of the will of God as the criterion of his undertakings, and who has not faith as the motivation of all that he does, is yet able to do what is right without qualification in certain areas of life.[4]

For Van Til, only the Christian theologian, who takes divinely inspired Scripture and the triune God of Christianity as his starting point, is able to approach what might be called a form of natural law.[5] Indeed, when it comes to knowledge and the study of anything "natural," Van Til states that "the truth of Christianity appears to be the immediately indispensable presupposition of the fruitful study of nature."[6] Karl Barth and Stanley Hauerwas,[7] simi-

---

[4] Cornelius Van Til, *Christian Apologetics*, ed. William Edgar, 2nd ed. (Phillipsburg, NJ: P&R Publishing, 2003), 38.

[5] Cornelius Van Til, *The Defense of the Faith*, ed. K. Scott Oliphint, 4th ed. (Phillipsburg, NJ: P&R Publishing, 2008), 78.

[6] Van Til, *Defense*, 279.

[7] Karl Barth, *Church Dogmatics*, trans. Bromiley, Campbell, Wilson, McNab, Knight, and Stewart, ed. Bromiley and Torrance (Peabody, MA: Hendrickson Publishers, 2010), II.2:528–35. Note, for example, Barth's comment to the effect that, "The order of obligation built on the order of being cannot as such be a real order of obligation, or at any rate of a divinely imperative obligation…. If obligation is grounded in being, this undoubtedly means that it is not grounded in itself, but ontically subordinated to another, and noetically to be derived from this other…. But on this presupposition it is quite impossible that it should confront him, his being and his existence with an absolute challenge; that it should dominate him and claim him with absolute sovereignty…." (Ibid., 532). Cf. Joseph L. Mangina, *Karl Barth: Theologian of*

larly, reject general revelation altogether, and natural law along with it. Others, such as Stanley Grenz, seem to think that natural law theory is refuted by the "so-called naturalistic fallacy",[8] and, therefore, reject it out of hand. Grenz later proposes that any form of natural law theory should be rejected, because "our pursuit of the true ethic requires that we reject the wisdom of the world—including the philosophical tradition."[9]

This hostility towards natural law is misplaced; as we will show in this book, natural law is both biblical and philosophically coherent. Indeed, the doctrine of natural law seems to be taught, not only by the Scriptures, but also by the Creeds and Confessions, and by great theologians throughout the history of the Church. Thus, the first section of this book explains the philosophical foundations of natural law, and the second section argues, in keeping with the predominant Protestant interpretation of Holy Scriptures, that the whole Bible presupposes and even teaches natural law.

Because the bulk of this book will be considering the biblical perspective of natural law, we will not belabor the point here. However, it is worth noting that Romans 2:14-

---

Christian Witness (Louisville, KY: Westminster John Knox Press, 2004), 146. Here Mangina notes that, for Barth, "There is no 'natural law', no minimal set of standards that applies to all human beings and that may be known apart from revelation. Barth rejects natural law for the same reason he rejects natural theology: both abstract from the concrete situation of the human being who lives under God's grace." Cf. Stanley Hauerwas, *The Peaceable Kingdom: A Primer in Christian Ethics* (Notre Dame, IN: University of Notre Dame Press, 1983), 63, 17.

[8] Stanley Grenz, *The Moral Quest: Foundations for Christian Ethics* (Downers Grove, IL: InterVarsity Press, 1997), 46. More on this later.

[9] Grenz, *The Moral Quest*, 163.

15 has been traditionally understood as teaching natural law:

> For when Gentiles, who do not have the law, by nature do what the law requires, they are a law to themselves, even though they do not have the law. They show that the work of the law is written on their hearts, while their conscience also bears witness, and their conflicting thoughts accuse or even excuse them. (Rom. 2:14-15)

We will explain, later, how this verse teaches natural law, but it will prove helpful, by way of introduction, to examine how some important Protestant theologians have approached these verses.

In his commentary on the Epistle to the Romans, John Calvin states that, in these verses, Paul "teaches us that they [the gentiles] carry, engraved on their hearts, a warning and judgment by which they discern between right and wrong, between honesty and villainy."[10] He continues: "Men, therefore, have a certain natural knowledge of the law, which teaches them and tells them, in themselves, that one thing is good, and the other detestable."[11] Calvin was

---

[10] Jehan Calvin, *Commentaires sur l'épistre aux Romains*, in tome 3 of *Commentaires de Jehan Calvin sur le Nouveau Testament* (Paris: Librairie de Ch. Meyrueis et co., 1855), 39. My translation. In French we read, « donnent à cognoistre qu'ils portent engrave en leurs cœurs un avis et jugement par lequel ils discernent entre le tort et le droict, entre honnesteté et vilenie. »

[11] Calvin, *Commentaires*, 40. My translation. In French we read, « Les hommes donc ont quelque intelligence naturelle de la Loy, laquelle intelligence les enseigne et leur dit en eux-mesmes qu'une chose est bonne, et l'autre détestable. »

not alone in interpreting these verses as referring to natural law; Martin Luther's commentary on Romans summarizes his answer to the question, "How do the Gentiles show that the work of the Law is written in their hearts?"[12] with the statement, "All of this proves that they know the Law by nature, or that they can distinguish between good and evil."[13] In fact, not only do Calvin and Luther understand Romans 2:14-15 to be speaking about natural human knowledge of true moral principles, but so do the great majority of important biblical exegetes, including but certainly not limited to, Origen,[14] Ambrosiaster,[15] John Chrysostom,[16] Thomas Aquinas,[17] Robert Haldane,[18] Charles Hodge,[19] John Murray,[20] F. F. Bruce,[21] Douglas

---

[12] Martin Luther, *Commentary on the Epistle to the Romans*, trans. J. Theodore Mueller (1954; repr., Grand Rapids: Kregel Publications, 1979), 60.

[13] Luther, *Commentary*, 60.

[14] Cf. J. Patout Burns, Jr., trans. and ed., *Romans: Interpreted by Early Christian Commentators* (Grand Rapids, MI: Wm. B. Eerdmans Publishing, 2012), 49–50.

[15] Burns, *Romans*, 46–47.

[16] Cf. Jean Chrysostome, *Homilies sur l'épître aux Romains*, vol. 8 des *Œuvres Complètes de S. Jean Chrysostome*, trans. Abbé J. Bareille (Paris: Librairie de Louis Vives, 1871), 252. Here he says, « Ce mot 'naturelle-ment' signifie l'application à suivre la raison naturelle. » My translation : "This word 'Naturally' signifies the effort to obey natural reason."

[17] Thomas Aquinas, *ST II-II*, Q. 94, A. 6. In the *Sed Contra* of this article Aquinas states, "the law that is written on the hearts of men is the Natural Law." This is, at once, a reference to a quote from Augustine, and a reference to Romans 2:14–15.

[18] Robert Haldane, *An Exposition of the Epistle to the Romans* (Florida: Mac Donald Publishing Company, 1958), 90.

[19] Charles Hodge, *A Commentary on Romans*, revised edition (1864; repr., Carlisle, PA: Banner of Truth Trust, 1975), 56-59. Hodge notes, in his section on the doctrine taught in these verses, that "The moral sense is

Moo,[22] Ben Witherington III,[23] and many others. It almost seems as if the denial of natural law within Protestant theology was more a result of the influence of the decline of the Aristotelian understanding of natural teleology and of the Kantian critique of reason, than of well-informed biblical interpretation.

Thus, not only does Scripture, as traditionally interpreted, teach natural law, but the great majority of Protestant theologians have found at least some place for natural law in their theology. Furthermore, the great Christian theologians from the second century down to the end of the Middle Ages taught natural law. Even most Puritan theologians firmly believed in natural law and appealed to natural law frequently in their theological treatises on various subjects.[24] The Anglican theologian Richard Hooker, a major opponent of the Puritans, concurred with their affirmation and defense of natural law.[25]

---

an original part of our constitution, and not the result of education" (Ibid., 58).

[20] John Murray, *The Epistle to the Romans* (Grand Rapids: Wm. B. Eerdmans Publishing, 1968), 72–79.

[21] F. F. Bruce, *The Epistle of Paul to the Romans: An Introduction and Commentary*, revised edition (1985; repr., Grand Rapids: Wm. B. Eerdmans Publishing, 2003), 84.

[22] Douglas Moo, *The Epistle to the Romans*, NICNT (Grand Rapids: Wm. B. Eerdmans Publishing, 1996), 148-153.

[23] Ben Witherington III and Darlene Hyatt, *Paul's Letter to the Romans: A Socio-Rhetorical Commentary* (Grand Rapids: Wm. B. Eerdmans Publishing, 2004), 73–84.

[24] Wallace W. Marshall, *Puritanism and Natural Theology* (Eugene, OR: Pickwick Publications, 2016), 22.

[25] Cf. Richard Hooker, *Divine Law and Human Nature: Or, the first book of Of the Laws of Ecclesiastical Polity, Concerning Laws and their Several Kinds in General*, ed./trans. W. Bradford Littlejohn, Brian Marr, and Bradley Belschner (Moscow, ID: The Davenant Press, 2017).

Perhaps most surprisingly, natural law made it into various Protestant creeds and confessions. The *Westminster Confession of Faith*, for example, seems to teach the doctrine of natural law when it states that

> there are some circumstances concerning the worship of God, and government of the Church, common to human actions and societies, which are to be ordered *by the light of nature* and Christian prudence, according to the general rules of the Word, which are always to be observed.[26]

The *Confessio Fidei Gallicana* (The French Confession of Faith), prepared by John Calvin, and delivered by Theodore Beza, is even more explicit. Here we read that fallen man "can still discern good and evil,"[27] without the help of Holy Scriptures.

We propose, therefore, that natural law is a necessary element of true Christian belief. We wish to invite the contemporary reader on a journey of discovery, in which we will introduce them to the philosophical foundations of and the Biblical teachings concerning natural law. We will demonstrate that natural law is both founded in human nature—as designed and created by God—and clearly taught in the Bible, the inspired Word of God.

---

[26] "The Westminster Confession of Faith, 1647," in Philip Schaff, *The Evangelical Protestant Creeds*, vol. 3 of *The Creeds of Christendom*, ed. David S. Schaff, 6th ed. (1983; repr., Grand Rapids: Baker Books, 2007), 604. Italics are mine. Cf. Ibid., 600.

[27] "The French Confession of Faith, A.D. 1559," in Philip Schaff, *The Evangelical Protestant Creeds*, vol. 3 of *The Creeds of Christendom*, ed. David S. Schaff, 6th ed. (1983; repr., Grand Rapids: Baker Books, 2007), 365.

PART I:
THE PHILOSOPHICAL FOUNDATIONS OF NATURAL LAW THEORY

I:

INTRODUCTION,
DISTINCTIONS AND DEFINITIONS

THE DOCTRINE of natural law can be found not only in the Bible, as we maintain in this book, but also in the writings of Plato, Aristotle, Cicero and the other Stoics, St. Augustine and most of the church fathers, Thomas Aquinas, and most pre-Kantian Reformed thinkers. Arthur F. Holmes suggests, rightly, that natural law theories depend, for their truth, upon the metaphysical theories which undergird them.[1] Two forms of natural law theory, founded on two very different ontologies, have been popular in the history of Christian moral thought: that of the Stoics and that of Aristotle.[2] The Stoic system finds the foundation for moral laws in reason alone, whereas the Aristotelian system finds the foundation for moral laws in the very nature of being (i.e., in human nature itself). In this section, we will consider the philosophical foundations of what we take to be a consistent Christian natural law theo-

---

[1] Arthur F. Holmes, *Ethics: Approaching Moral Decisions* (Downers Grove, IL: InterVarsity Press, 1984), 63.

[2] Holmes, *Ethics*, 62.

ry—that which flows out of Aristotelian metaphysics. We will begin by making a number of distinctions and definitions. We will then go into greater detail concerning the two metaphysical foundations of natural law, and, finally, some epistemological elements of natural law, which flow out of the metaphysical foundations. We hope to show that a coherent natural law theory depends upon a particular philosophical position, and, secondly, that this philosophical position and the natural law theory which it supports are defensible.

We must first provide a proper definition of natural law. To do this, we must understand the various elements which go into its definition. First of all, *Nature*, or *Natural*, has come to mean many different things. It may refer at least (a) to the way in which a thing normally acts (whether this be the normal attitudes, actions, and reactions of a human individual; the normal actions of some created but non-rational thing; or even the normal actions of an artifact, or otherwise non-sentient thing—such as the "sin nature"); (b) to the personality, character, or identity of rational (or quasi-rational) beings; (c) to the created universe, including human beings; (d) to the created universe in exclusion of human beings; or (e) to the "that which something is," which not only determines how we classify the something in question, but which also determines how that something acts and develops over time (this is sometimes called the "essence"). In natural law theory, the term *natural* refers to that which makes X to be X and not something other than X. This has frequently been referred to as the *nature* of X, the *essence* of X, or the *form* of X.

The term "law" likewise admits of many definitions. It may refer to a *descriptive* statement, which tells us what every X *will* do in certain circumstances. We talk about the law of gravity, for example. In natural law theory, though, "law" refers to a *normative* dictum which tells us what every X *should* do, in certain circumstances. Note that in the case of a descriptive law, we are describing how X always acts; but, in the case of a normative law we are describing how X should, but may not, act. Thomas Aquinas provides us with the following definition of a normative law, "Law is a rule and measure of acts, whereby man is induced to act or is restrained from acting."[3]

J. Budziszewski sums up the preceding observations well,

> Law may be defined as an ordinance of reason, for the common good, made by him who has care of the community, and promulgated. Nature may be conceived as an ensemble of things with particular natures, and a thing's nature may be thought of as the design imparted to it by the Creator—in traditional language, as a purpose implanted in it by the divine art, that it be moved to a determinate end. The claim of the theory is that in exactly

---

[3] Thomas Aquinas, *Summa Theologiae, I-II, Q. 90, A. 1*, trans. Fathers of the English Dominican Province (Notre Dame, IN: Ave Maria Press, 1948), 2:993. All other quotations from the *Summa Theologiae*, unless otherwise noted, will be from this translation, and will be referenced, according to the traditional method, as follows: *ST*, Pt…, Q…, A…

these senses, Natural Law is both (1) true law, and (2) truly expressive of nature.[4]

By *natural law*, then, we mean that order or rule of human conduct which is (1) based upon human nature as created by God, (2) knowable by all men, through human intuition and reasoning alone (beginning from his observations of creation, in general, and human nature, in particular), independent of any particular divine revelation provided through a divine spokesperson; and, thus (3) normative for all human beings. Jacques Maritain seems to agree with this definition, as he notes that

> the genuine concept of natural law is the concept of a law which is natural not only insofar as it expresses the normality of functioning of human nature, but also insofar as it is naturally known, that is, known through inclination or through connaturality, not through conceptual knowledge and by way of reasoning.[5]

Note that Maritain also distinguishes between two aspects that must be involved in any genuine theory of natural law: (1) the *metaphysical* element—immutable natures upon which natural law is based, and (2) the *epistemological* element—the way in which in humans obtain knowledge of natural law.

---

[4] J. Budziszewski, *The Line Through the Heart: Natural Law as Fact, Theory, and Sign of Contradiction* (Wilmington, DE: ISI Books, 2011), 10-11. See also Ralph McInerny, "Ethics," in *The Cambridge Companion to Aquinas*, ed. Norman Kretzmann and Eleonore Stump (Cambridge: Cambridge University Press, 2005), 209.

[5] Jacques Maritain, *Natural Law: Reflections on Theory and Practice*, ed. William Sweet (South Bend, IN: St. Augustine's Press, 2001), 20.

In order to avoid any misinterpretations, it will be helpful to distinguish natural law from three other types of law which are frequently discussed in Christian literature: eternal law, *jus gentium*, and positive law. natural law is not co-extensive with what many Christian theologians call *eternal law*. eternal law is, so to speak, no less than the ideas in the mind of God, of all that exists, as they are applied to the direction of all things. The eternal law does not stand over God; it is nothing more than the Divine essence—the ultimate Good itself, which is God, and towards which all things tend.[6] Thomas Aquinas argues to this definition by noting both that every creator has the idea of that which he wishes to make, prior to making it, and that every governor has the idea of the order that he wishes to impose, prior to creating order:

> Now God, by His wisdom, is the Creator of all things in relation to which He stands as the artificer to the products of his art…. Moreover He governs all the acts and movements that are to be found in each single creature…Wherefore as the type of the Divine Wisdom, inasmuch as by It all things are created, has the character of art, exemplar or idea; so the type of Divine Wisdom, as moving all things to their due ends, bears the character of law. Accordingly the eternal law

---

[6] Michael Baur, "Law and Natural Law," in *The Oxford Handbook of Aquinas*, ed. Brian Davies & Eleonore Stump (Oxford: Oxford University Press, 2014), 245–46.

is nothing else than the type of Divine Wisdom, as directing all actions and movements.[7]

Thus, the eternal law is the very mind of God as it is applied to His sovereign ordering and governing of creation.[8] It should become obvious, therefore, that eternal law is not, in an unqualified sense, natural law, for (1) man cannot know the mind of God, neither by intuition, nor by any reasoning process, but man can know the natural law, and (2) though the natural law finds its basis in the eternal law, eternal law is not based upon the created natures, but rather is the Divine mind from which all created natures flow. Though we can distinguish between natural law and eternal law, we must maintain, along with Michael Baur, that

> the natural law is the eternal law itself, but regarded under the aspect of its being in us (rational beings) in this unique, twofold way: it is in us as in created beings that are ruled, measured, and directed by means of it, but also in us as in created (rational) beings that rule, measure, and direct (both ourselves and other things) by means of it.[9]

As such, eternal law is foundational for natural law, just as the mind of the inventor is foundational for the purpose and working of his invention. The French Dominican A.G. Sertillanges summarizes this point well, "*Natural law*

---

[7] Aquinas, *ST*, I-II, Q. 93, A. 1.

[8] Richard Hooker would appear to agree with our definition of eternal law (cf. Hooker, *Divine Law and Human Nature*, 5, 8).

[9] Baur, "Law and Natural Law," 246.

is defined as: *a participation in the eternal law, an impression of the divine light in the rational creature, by which it is inclined to right action*, that is, towards that action which accomplishes its end."[10]

Neither may natural law be equated with *human law* (for which "positive law" may be taken as a synonym). As Jacques Maritain notes, there are two important differences between natural law and human law: (1) human law is produced by reason's application of general principles to particular cases for the common good; and (2) the author of human law is man—who decides or discovers what laws must be installed in a particular society for the common good of the citizens of that society.[11] It should be evident, then, that natural law is not human law, but, that it should be foundational for human law.

With these distinctions, then, we see that (1) natural law is founded upon the natures of created beings—specifically, for our purposes, human beings—as those natures were created by God; (2) natural law participates in the eternal law; (3) natural law should be the basis of human law; (4) natural law is in principle knowable by human beings; and (5) natural law is normative for all human beings.

It is also worth noting, first of all, that natural law is neither *mechanistic* nor *without exception*.[12] Secondly, to say

---

[10] A.G. Sertillanges, *La Philosophie Morale de St. Thomas d'Aquin*, 2e ed. (Paris: Éditions Montaigne, 1946), 100. My translation. In French we read, « la *loi naturelle* se définit : *une participation de la loi éternelle, une impression de la lumière divine dans la créature raisonnable, par laquelle elle est inclinée à l'action droite*, c'est-à-dire à l'action qui peut réaliser sa fin. »

[11] Maritain, *Natural Law: Reflections on Theory and Practice*, 48–49.

[12] Thank you to Andrew Fulford for bringing up these important distinctions. He noted that "the error suggesting that Natural Law must

that there is a natural law which is knowable by even. generate human beings is not, as some theologians have wrongly claimed, to say that humans are autonomous or independent of God. Van Til, for example, famously argues that one of the primary characterizations of the unregenerate person is that he sees himself as autonomous.[13] For Van Til, to be autonomous means, in part at least, that man needs no revelation. He states, for example, that "The revelation of a self-sufficient God can have no meaning for a mind that thinks of itself as ultimately autonomous."[14] In the following paragraph, he writes that,

> If man is in any sense autonomous, he is not in need of revelation. If he is then said to possess the truth, he possesses it as the product of the ultimately legislative powers of his intellect. It is only if he can virtually control by means of the application of the law of non-contradiction all the facts of reality that surround him, that he can know any truth at all. And thus, if he knows any truth in this way, he, in effect, knows all truth.[15]

---

be without exception to be real is sometimes implied not by those who accept the idea, but those who reject it. An example is found in Christine Gudorf's paper 'The Erosion of Sexual Dimorphism,' where she argues that the contemporary discoveries of numerous variations in gender, sex, and sexuality implies dimorphism has been refuted by science." Cf. "The Erosion of Sexual Dimorphism," *Journal of the American Academy of Religion* 69, no. 4 (Dec. 2001): 867.

[13] Cf. Van Til, *Christian Apologetics*, 79.

[14] Van Til, *Defense*, 112.

[15] Van Til, *Defense*, 112.

But, says Van Til, describing the approach of Thomas Aquinas to naturally known truths,

> Following Aristotle's method of reasoning, Thomas Aquinas argues that the natural man can, by the ordinary use of his reason, do justice to the natural revelation that surrounds him … the natural man is already in possession of the truth. To be sure, he is said to be in possession of the truth only with respect to natural revelation."[16]

And, continues Van Til, if man knows truth naturally, then he is autonomous and does not need divine revelation.[17] It follows that, for Van Til, natural law theory is based upon the notion of autonomy—that man is ultimately autonomous and not in need of God. However, as even a cursory study of the works of Thomas Aquinas will show, those who see a place for natural law within classical Christian theology are also ardent defenders of man's absolute dependence on God, not only for human nature and the existence of individual humans, but, also, for the salvation of mankind.

What we have seen thus far leads us to distinguish three important aspects of natural law, two of which are foundational: (1) the divine foundation of natural law, (2) the metaphysical foundation of natural law, and (3) the epistemological aspects of natural law. It is to the exploration of these three aspects that we now turn.

---

[16] Van Til, *Christian Apologetics*, 111.

[17] Van Til, *Christian Apologetics*, 111–12.

II:

THE DIVINE FOUNDATION OF NATURAL LAW

GOD AND NATURAL LAW

HUGO GROTIUS is famous for fathering what would become modern natural law theory.[1] He is also famous, unfortunately, for having posited that even if God did not exist, natural law would.[2] As we consider the divine foundation of natural law, we will contend the contrary. It should be noted, both by way of introduction to this section, and to do justice to the thought of Grotius, that he

---

[1] Cf. Steven Forde, "Hugo Grotius on Ethics and War," *American Political Science Review* 92, no. 3 (Sept. 1998): 639-640. William Rattigan, "Hugo Grotius," *Journal of the Society of Comparative Legislation* 6, no. 1 (1905): 78.

[2] Hugo Grotius, *On the Rights of War and Peace: An Abridged Translation*, trans. and ed. William Whewell (Cambridge: John W. Parker, 1853), xxvi. Grotius famously said, "And what we have said would still have great weight, even if we were to grant, what we cannot grant without wickedness, that there is no God, or that he bestows no regard on human affairs." Cf. Maritain, *Natural Law*, 46. Carl F. H. Henry, "Natural Law and a Nihilistic Culture," *First Things* (January 1995), www.firstthings.com/article/1995/01/natural-law-and-a-nihilistic-culture (accessed 2017-08-19).

also stated natural law essentially presupposes the existence of God and that it finds its ultimate foundation in God, who made human nature in this way.[3] The first metaphysical foundation of natural law, as Grotius almost reluctantly admitted, is God Himself. We propose that if God did not exist, *contra* Grotius, then neither would natural law. We will here consider what it means to say that God is the foundation of natural law.

The notion of a normative "law," as is proposed in natural law theory, implies no less than: (1) a rational standard which is enforced, and (2) a being who both imposes and enforces that law—thus a rational and powerful being. A law which was irrational but enforced would rightly draw both critique and rebellion. A law which was rational but not enforced would be pointless and would only draw ridicule to the Lawmaker. Consider, for example, creating the following rule for soccer: a player must "stop, drop, and roll" every time he or she receives or intercepts a pass. This rule would immediately draw the ire of all soccer players, who would in turn rightly rebel against the lawmaker for rendering the sport impossible to play. On the other hand, it is entirely rational to impose speed limits for safe driving speeds on highways and city

---

[3] Grotius argues that natural law is founded upon human nature, as it was made by God (Cf. Forde, "Hugo Grotius," 640). In Grotius's *On the Rights of War and Peace*, we read, "And here we are brought to another origin of Jus, besides that natural source; namely, the free will of God, to which, as our reason irresistibly tells us, we are bound to submit ourselves. But even that Natural Law of which we have spoken, whether it be that which binds together communities, or that looser kind [which enjoins duties,] although it do proceed from the internal principles of man, may yet be rightly ascribed to God; because it was by His will that such principles came to exist in us" (Grotius, *On the Rights of War and Peace*, xxvi).

streets; because this law is rarely enforced, however, an unspoken law—according to which one may drive faster than the limit—was gradually accepted, by which it became permissible to drive faster than the limit, and to ridicule or despise those who do not. The very notion of a normative law, therefore, necessitates a rational law-maker who is able to enforce the law.[4]

Now, as stated above, natural law is said to be an order or rule of human conduct which is based upon the divinely created human nature and which is normative for all human beings. By its very definition, then, natural law assumes the existence of a superior being which is (1) the creator of human nature, or, at least, the governor of all human beings, (2) the rational author of the (natural) law which applies to human beings, and (3) the powerful enforcer of this law. In other words, if there is a natural law, then there is a Being which is superior to Human-beings, which is rational, and which is powerful enough to enforce the standard He has imposed upon the beings He governs. Before asking whether there is such a Being, it should be noted that the relationship stated above does not go both ways. That is, the existence of God does not entail the existence of natural law. It is true that God's existence entails eternal law, but in order for natural law to exist, there must be more than just God. In the first place, in order for there to be natural law, there must be a creation.

---

[4] Richard Hooker would seem to agree with this statement. He states, for example, that "Nearly everything works according to a law subject to some superior, who has authored it; only the works and operations of God have Him as both their worker and as their law. The very being of God is a sort of law to His working, for the perfection that God is, gives perfection to what God does" (Hooker, *Divine Law and Human Nature*, 4–5).

If there is a God but no created universe, then there is certainly eternal law; but the concept of natural law would have no referent other than the divine nature, and, thus, natural law would be co-extensive with (and therefore identical with) eternal law. There would be no natural law if there were no creatures.

Not even the existence of a created universe necessarily provides us with natural law. In fact, even if there were both a divine being and a created universe, if there were no immutable natures or essences, then there would be no natural law. One might, for example, hold to a form of metaphysical nominalism, thus suggesting that there are no created natures or essences.[5] If there are no created natures or essences, then there can be no natural law, at least, not as we have defined it. The only theory possible for a nominalist metaphysics is a form of divine command

---

[5] Nominalism (in all its varieties) is anti-essentialist—it denies the existence of real essences and universals. Nominalism is often, though not without debate, linked primarily to Guillaume of Ockham, who certainly presented one of the strongest defenses of Nominalism to come out of the high Middle ages and who is often portrayed as the father of modern Nominalism. Others, such as Philotheus Bohner and Marilyn McCord-Adams, appear to argue that Ockham is much more of a Realist than he is frequently portrayed; cf. Philotheus Bohner, "The Realistic Conceptualism of William Ockham," *Traditio* 4 (1946): 307–35; Marilyn McCord-Adams, "Ockham's Nominalism and Unreal Entities," *The Philosophical Review* 86, no. 2 (April 1977): 152. It seems best to maintain that Ockham was indeed a Nominalist, following Alain De Libera, nominalist and Ockham scholar, who points out that if realism can be defined so loosely as to posit that Ockham is a realist, then we really have no precise definition of just what qualifies as realism. Cf. Alain De Libera, "Question de réalisme. Sur deux arguments anti-ockhamistes de John Sharpe," *Revue de Métaphysique et de Morale* 97e Année, No. 1, Les Universaux (Janvier-mars 1992): 85. Claiming that Ockham was a realist simply blurs the lines between Realism and Nominalism (and Ockham's particular form of Nominalism frequently called Conceptualism).

theory; that is, if a nominalist metaphysics is true, then there can only be divine command, and no natural law (for there are no natures upon which natural law would be based or to which it could apply).[6] Suffice it to say that, at the very least, if there is a divine creator (implying creation), then there is also a divinely imposed law of some sort. But, is there a divine creator?

Peter Kreeft, in his book *Making Sense out of Suffering*, states that

> there may be one very good argument against God—evil—but there are many more good arguments for God. In fact, there are at least fifteen different arguments for God…. Atheists must answer all fifteen arguments; theists must answer only one.[7]

But, says Kreeft, interestingly enough, "The very existence of evil proves the existence of God."[8] Kreeft goes on to show, based upon the very existence of evil in the universe, the existence of moral or spiritual evil, and the very

---

[6] In his chapter on the Nominalist explosion of the late middle ages, Servais Pinckaers notes that natural law had to be reinterpreted in light of the rejection of Realism, "Ockham maintained the existence of Natural Law (for this was imposed upon him by scholastic tradition), but he reinterpreted it in keeping with his own system. Natural law was no longer based, for him, on human nature and its inclinations, which reason could reveal. It consisted rather in the authority of right reason presenting directly to the human will the orders and obligations that emanated from the divine will, without there being any need whatsoever to justify them, since the justification of the law could be found only in the divine will itself." Cf. *The Sources of Christian Ethics*, 3rd ed., trans. Mary Thomas Noble (Washington, D.C: CUA Press, 1995), 248–49.

[7] Peter Kreeft, *Making Sense out of Suffering* (Ann Arbor, MI: Servant Books, 1986), 30.

[8] Kreeft, *Making Sense*, 30.

idea of evil, that God exists.[9] To these arguments we might add the five ways of Thomas Aquinas, which, beginning with change, efficient causality, contingent beings, degrees of goodness and justice, and obvious tendencies, in irrational and nonvolitional beings, to always pursue the same ends, can be used to demonstrate the existence of a creator God who is the unchanging cause of all change, the first efficient cause from which all causality flows, a being which is necessary by it's very nature, self-subsistent Goodness, Truth, Justice, etc., and, finally, that this same God is the intelligent Creator who governs the entirety of creation, directing each being to its proper end. That this universe was created by God, therefore, is evident.

Though it is not necessary to elaborate on each of these arguments it may be felicitous to briefly outline an argument which may trace its roots all the way to Paul's speech at Lystra, where he says,

> Men, why are you doing these things? We also are men, of like nature with you, and we bring you good news, that you should turn from these vain things to a living God, who made the heaven and the earth and the sea and all that is in them. In past generations he allowed all the nations to walk in their own ways. Yet he did not leave himself without witness, for he did good by giving you rains from heaven and fruitful seasons, satisfying your hearts with food and gladness. (Acts 14:15–17)

---

[9] Kreeft, *Making Sense*, 31.

These verses have traditionally been understood as supporting the notion that man can know of God's providential governance of this world through his observations of the natural world.

Many important theologians throughout the history of the Church have proposed just this type of argument. Speaking of the unbeliever, Gregory of Nyssa says, in his *Great Catechism*,

> Should he say there is no God, then, from the consideration of the skilful and wise economy of the Universe he will be brought to acknowledge that there is a certain overmastering power manifested through these channels.[10]

His close friend Gregory of Nazianzus presents the same argument in his treatise *On Theology*, where he says, "Now our own eyes and the Law of Nature teach us that God exists, and that He is both the creative Cause of all things and the Cause-that-maintains-all-things-in-harmony."[11] In the *Institutes*, Calvin says,

> Since the perfection of blessedness consists in the knowledge of God, he has been pleased, in order that none might be excluded from the means of obtaining felicity ... to manifest his perfections in the whole structure of the universe, and daily place himself in our view,

---

[10] Gregory of Nyssa, *The Great Catechism*, in Series 2 of the *Nicene and Post-Nicene Fathers*, ed. Philip Schaff (NY: Christian Literature Publishing, 1892), 5:474.

[11] Gregory of Nazianzus, *On Theology*, in *Five Theologial Orations*, trans. Stephen Reynolds (Estate of Stephen Reynolds, 2011), 18.

> that we cannot open our eyes without being compelled to behold him.[12]

He continues, a little later,

> I only wish to observe here, that this method of investigating the divine perfections, by tracing the lineaments of his countenance as shadowed forth in the firmament and on the earth, is common both to those within and to those without the pale of the church.[13]

These perfections are evident when we consider the things that God has made, where we observe, according to Calvin, God's power, eternity, self-existence, goodness, providence, divine wisdom and majesty.[14] Though Calvin does not posit any one argument, he allows that there are such arguments, and points the reader to those scholars who have offered them,

> In attestation of his wonderous wisdom, both the heavens and the earth present us with innumerable proofs, not only those more recondite proofs which astronomy, medicine, and all the natural sciences are designed to illustrate, but proofs which force themselves on the notice of the most illiterate peasant,

---

[12] John Calvin, *Institutes of the Christian Religion*, trans. Henry Beveridge (2008; repr., Peabody, MA: Hendrickson Publishers, 2012), 16.

[13] Calvin, *Institutes*, 20.

[14] Calvin, *Institutes*, 20–21.

who cannot open his eyes without beholding them.[15]

These proofs are so abundant, and evident to all men (regenerate and unregenerate alike), that Calvin states, "Hence it is obvious, that in seeking God, the most direct path and the fittest method is ... to contemplate him in his works, by which he draws near, becomes familiar, and in a manner communicates himself to us."[16]

Perhaps the clearest summary of this type of argument can be found in Aquinas's *Summa Theologiae* where Aquinas argues in his "fifth way" of demonstrating God's existence that

> We see that things which lack intelligence, such as natural bodies, tend towards an end.... But, those things which do not have intelligence, do not tend towards an end unless directed by a thing that is both knowing and intelligent, as the arrow is directed by the archer. There is, therefore, an intelligent being, by which all natural things are directed towards an end: and this we call God.[17]

This argument, which is rather simple, simply notes that we observe things in the natural world which always tend towards the same end: ears tend to receive sound, eyes tend to receive refracted light, animals tend towards easily obtained food, and so on. But, these things are not intelligent beings. They do not choose their pursued goals,

---

[15] Calvin, *Institutes*, 16–17.

[16] Calvin, *Institutes*, 21.

[17] Aquinas, *ST I*, Q. 2, A. 3, *Respondeo*.

but seemingly act without intelligent choice. But, when we observe something that always tends towards the same goal without intelligent choice, we attribute this consistent movement to some directing intelligence. The directing intelligence of the world, that being which providentially governs all natural beings so that they consistently pursue their natural ends, is what we call God. The providential government of the world demonstrates that a divine Creator exists. It follows, therefore, that there is some sort of standard which this Creator holds over His creation. In other words, God, therefore, law.

IMPLICATIONS OF DIVINE CREATION

Before we move on to the second metaphysical foundation which is necessary for natural law, we should ask how God created. This may, in fact, provide a hint to just what type of law we can expect to find. We propose that part of the answer to this question can be found in Aquinas's response to the question "Whether the Knowledge of God is the Cause of Things?", where he states,

> The knowledge of God is the cause of things. For the knowledge of God is to all creatures what the knowledge of the artificer is to things made by his art. Now the knowledge of the artificer is the cause of the things made by his art from the fact that the artificer works by his intellect.[18]

Now, this seems elementary: if God is the creator of everything, then it is obvious that His divine knowledge causes

---

[18] Aquinas, *ST* I, q. 14, A. 8, *Respondeo.*

creation. Yet this reveals something crucial about creation and its relationship to God.

When a carpenter builds a table, he is doing on a small scale what God did on a universal scale. That is, the carpenter begins with an idea of what the finished product will look like, and then, through the construction process, brings that idea to fruition. In the same way, the created universe was the physical production of divine ideas—God "began" with an idea of what the finished product would look like, and brought (and is bringing) it to fruition. Aquinas notes that "Ideas are types existing in the divine mind, as is clear from Augustine. But God has the proper types of all things that He knows; and therefore He has ideas of all things known by Him."[19] Aquinas goes on to state that "As ideas, according to Plato, are principles of the knowledge of things and of their generation, an idea has this twofold office, as it exists in the mind of God. So far as the idea is the principle of the making of things, it may be called an *exemplar*, and belongs to practical knowledge. But so far as it is a principle of knowledge, it is properly called a *type*, and may belong to speculative knowledge also."[20] The exemplar cause just is the standard to which each created thing is held, and by which it is measured. Just as the carpenter judges his finished table by the idea of the table that he conceived in his mind.

We propose, then, that God is the first foundation of natural law, and this in a twofold manner: (1) First of all, as the creator of everything, nothing was brought into existence which was not caused by God; thus, God is the crea-

---

[19] Aquinas, *ST* I, q. 15, A. 3, *Sed Contra*.

[20] Aquinas, *Respondeo*.

tor of man, and has established a moral standard over man. (2) Secondly, as the creator of everything, the idea of each and every thing is to be found, as that thing is meant to be, in the mind of God—as exemplar causes of the things that exist. This prepares us for, and leads us into, the broader metaphysical foundation of natural law.

III:

THE METAPHYSICAL FOUNDATION
OF NATURAL LAW

THE DIVINE foundation of natural law brings us to an interesting conclusion: the divine mind "contains," or is, the ideas of all created beings—what we call exemplar causes—in much the same way that the carpenter's mind contains the idea of the finished table prior to beginning his work. These exemplar causes are just what Plato and Augustine called the eternal *Ideas* or *Forms*, and what Aquinas called, as we have already seen, the exemplars of all created beings. This provides us with a great introduction to the second metaphysical foundation of natural law: the combination of metaphysical and epistemological Realism which we will call *Moderate Realism.*

To say that Moderate Realism is the foundation of natural law is to say that natural law is based upon two principles: (1) created essences exist, and (2) essences can be known. As we noted above, if there are no eternal essences, then there is no "natural" law; there may be a law, but it is not natural, i.e., based upon created essences. In this section, we will attempt, first of all, to show how we arrive at the conclusion that there are created essences (that is, we will attempt to motivate the reader to accept the existence of essences), and secondly, we will show how the existence of created essences necessitates natural law.

GETTING TO CREATED NATURES

There are many reasons to accept the existence of essences. First, the natural sciences, both in the way in which they carry out their research, and in the discoveries they make, assume the existence of essences.[1] In addition, philosophical dialogue of all sorts seems incapable of denying the existence of essences, without either using extremely obtuse language with no connection to reality or claiming that, though we talk as if there are real essences, our language betrays us.[2] Indeed, Plato seems to claim that if we deny the existence of essences—the Forms—then we have, at the same time, denied the very possibility of dialogue and philosophy.[3] So, all anti-essentialist philosophies end up being anti-philosophy philosophies! In what follows, we will attempt to provide something of an idea of how we come to recognize the existence of essences—one might call it a phenomenology of human knowledge of essences.

When we look around us we are impressed by the great variety of existing things: cars, houses, trees, dogs, cats, humans, mountains, and valleys. We are less, though

---

[1] Cf. Edward Feser, *Scholastic Metaphysics: A Contemporary Introduction* (Germany: Editionses Scholasticae, 2014), 213–15.

[2] Cf. Feser, *Scholastic Metaphysics*, 215. Oderberg, *Real Essentialism* (New York: Routledge, 2007), 38–43.

[3] Plato, *Parmenides*, trans. Mary Louise Gill and Paul Ryan (Indianapolis, IN: Hackett, 1996), 138 [135b-c].

perhaps wrongly, impressed by the fact that there are so many things of the same "type," that we are able to talk about such things in general terms. Each of these words picks out whole groups of entities which, though distinct, resemble each other enough that we can group them together under types or species.

From conception to death we are constantly encountering beings of different types. As children, we touch everything we can, put everything in our mouths, and play games like "which of these things is not like the other?" In doing this, we are distinguishing between different types of beings, classifying them according to shape, colour, taste, the sounds they make, etc. We come into contact with things that move when we touch them, with things that only move when we make them move, and with things that move us (into bed, out of bed, into a baby seat, etc.). As we grow older, we begin classifying these things differently. We realize that there is a difference between the toy dog and the pet dog, between the flower and the frog, between the cat and our brother or sister. We are able to distinguish between the animate, the inanimate, and the human.

As we grow still older we begin asking questions about the things we have known, for so long, through our senses. We are already aware of the differences, but we want to know—what do we call these things? What are they? Perhaps surprisingly, this question can be answered in many different ways. The most obvious, the way which is used by parents to help young children distinguish between the different things, is linguistic. A word is provided which signifies, or points towards, things of that type, i.e., cat, dog, horse. Parents do this with their children as they read books which have pictures of different animals, shapes, or colours. But there is more.

If I look at a house, and I ask, "what is it?", you could respond by giving me a list of the materials used in its construction: wood, rocks, cement, metal, etc. Though this answer is both true and accurate, it is usually not the answer we are looking for when we ask the "what is it?" question. You might also respond by pointing out that it is the creation of some very well-known architect. This answer, though also true and accurate, is also usually not the answer we are looking for. You might also respond by giving me the type of answer we are usually looking for when we ask the "what is it?" question: that is, either the name, which is a quick way of designating its definition—"it is a 'house'"—or the reason for its existence—"it is a shelter." Note that these different answers, all of which are true and accurate, pick out what Aristotle and Aquinas are talking about when they refer to the material, efficient, formal, and final causes of a thing.[4]

Our observation of these causes, especially the formal cause, give us what we call the essence or nature of the thing.[5] Thomas Aquinas, in his short treatise *De Ente et*

---

[4] The material cause refers to that of which a thing is made or composed. The efficient cause refers to the proximate agent or event which brought about the thing in question. The formal cause refers to the nature or essence of the thing. The final cause refers to the "raison d'être" of the thing—that for which the thing exists.

[5] There have been many attempts to refute the existence of natures. We cannot, due to space constraints, consider these attempts. For responses to most anti-essentialist arguments, we refer the reader to David S. Oderberg, *Real Essentialism*; Henry Veatch, *Realism and Nominalism Revisited* (Milwaukee, WI: Marquette University Press, 1954); Étienne Gilson, *Being and Some Philosophers*, 2nd ed. (Toronto, ON: Pontifical Institute of Mediaeval Studies, 1952); and Edward Feser, *Scholastic Metaphysics*, 211–16.

Essentia, states that, first of all, "essence must mean something common to all the natures through which different beings are placed in different genera and species."[6] The *nature*, then, as related to a substance,[7] "seems to mean the essence of a thing as directed to its specific operation, for no reality lacks its specific operation."[8] Etienne Gilson adds to this that "of course, we know that, in the Aristotelian sense, 'nature' is the inner and direct source of the activity and doings of any being."[9] We see, then, that the nature of a thing will be its formal cause. It is also worth noting that the final cause and the formal cause of a thing are so closely related that the formal cause of a thing always seems to be conceived in terms of that thing's final cause (its end, its purpose). It follows, then, that the nature of a thing seems to include its final cause. As we noted above, the formal cause of a thing is the proper definition of the thing—and the definition of the thing picks out that which most distinguishes that thing from everything else.

A SHORT EPISTEMOLOGICAL EXCURSUS

Three points must be made before we move on if we are to avoid possible misunderstandings. First, when we come

---

[6] Thomas Aquinas, *On Being and Essence*, trans. Armand Maurer, 2nd ed. (Toronto, ON: PIMS, 1968), 30.

[7] It is important to note here that the word "substance" as used by Aquinas, refers to Aristotle's term οὐσίας (pronounced *ousias*), which, for Aristotle, refers primarily to an existing essence (not to some unknowable substructure, or to some idea in the mind, but to the existing instantiated essence which is observable by the senses).

[8] Aquins, *On Being*, 32.

[9] Etienne Gilson, *Moral Values and the Moral Life: The Ethical Theory of St. Thomas Aquinas*, trans. Leo Richard Ward (Hamden, CT: The Shoe String Press, 1961), 55.

across a human invention for the first time, we are often able to figure out what it is made of (material cause), who made it (efficient cause), but, what mystifies us, more often than not, is why the inventor made it—that is, what is it for (final cause)? Sometimes we try to guess at its purpose based upon its material causality, or based upon some aspect of the invention (such as its shape, colour, or parts). Until we discover what the human invention was made *for*, we do not know *what it is*. We can discover what the invention is *for* in one of two ways: (1) finding out, by experience, what it *does*, that is—what is the primary activity or effect of the invention[10] or (2) asking the inventor. This can be applied just as well to created beings. To discover what a human being is, we need to ask about the purpose of human beings. To discover their purpose, we can either discover by experience the primary activity of human beings, or we can ask the creator. Note that what we *call* the invention (the word or small phrase by which we refer to the invention) does not actually play a role in telling us what it is—its "nature." Rather, the name is typically given to the invention because of what it is—human language is logically posterior to created natures and our knowledge of them.

Secondly, we do not need to know everything about the invention to know what the invention is. Typically, we only need to know what it is *for* to know what it *is*. For

---

[10] I say "primary activity or effect" in distinction from secondary or tertiary effects. For example, many medicines often have a primary effect (for example, preventing some sickness), but also cause many secondary effects (such as vomiting, dry throat, depression, etc.). Finding the secondary effects or activities of something will not tell you what that thing is for. Only the primary effect or activity of the thing can tell you what that thing is for.

example, when we discover that some machine has been built with the purpose of preserving food by means of removing all warmth, we discover the nature of the machine (and we call it, in English, a fridge). Coming to know the purpose of the invention is sufficient for grasping its nature. We don't need to know how it works, how each part fits into the overall working of the machine, etc. This information may be interesting, and, by reverse engineering we may come to be amazed at the ingenuity of the inventor, but this extra information is not necessary for learning the nature of the invention. David Oderberg, in *Real Essentialism*, notes that, in relation to gold,

> the ultimate explanation, for the essentialist, of why gold behaves as it does is *not* that it falls under even more *general* classifications and so is susceptible of explanation by theories at those higher levels, but that it falls under the *most specific* characterization possible for it. In other words, ultimate explanation is not explanation in terms of the most general, but precisely the opposite—explanation in terms of the most specific. The most specific characterization is what marks gold off from everything else in the universe and so explains the features that give it its particular identity in the scheme of reality.[11]

So, with humans, for example, we need not know everything about their inner workings, to be able to arrive at an understanding of human nature. We "simply" need

---

[11] David S. Oderberg, *Real Essentialism* (New York: Routledge, 2007), 34.

to land upon that which distinguishes humans from everything else of their type.

Thirdly, regardless of whether one thinks, like Maritain, that human knowledge of natural law is a connatural knowledge,[12] or whether one thinks that we come to knowledge of the truths of natural law through inferential reasoning, it is obvious that most human beings do not seem to rationally arrive at very specific moral laws. They may light upon some very general moral laws, as C. S. Lewis so easily shows in the *Abolition of Man*,[13] but most humans have trouble both knowing the good in more specific situations and in obeying even those general moral principles that they know. We might say, then, to borrow Aquinas's statement about the necessity of divine revelation in relation to human knowledge of God, that as concerns even those truths that man could know about what is morally good,

> it was necessary that man should be taught by a divine revelation; because [those moral truths] such as reason could discover would only be known by a few, and that after a long time, and with the admixture of many errors.[14]

---

[12] Connatural knowledge is essentially knowledge by intuition or affection. It is that knowledge which man seems to hold without having consciously thought about the subject in question.

[13] C. S. Lewis, *The Abolition of Man* (New York: HarperOne, 2000). See, specifically, the Appendix—Illustrations of the Tao.

[14] Aquinas, *ST* I, Q. 1, A. 1, *Respondeo*.

So, the Word of God reveals even those truths about human morality which can be known naturally, that is, which are based upon human nature itself.[15]

This brings us to ask the question: what are human-beings?

FROM CREATED ESSENCES TO NATURAL LAW

What are Humans?

Aquinas notes that "the definition telling what a thing is signifies that by which a thing is located in its genus or species."[16] The definition of human-being, then, is an animal (genus) that is rational (specific difference). Human beings are animals because they are biological, animate beings which contain within themselves the source of their own movement, and which are capable of sensorial interaction with their environment. Human beings are human—i.e. distinguished from all other animals—because they are rational.

Of course, many other distinguishing features could be proposed: man is a social being, created in God's image, able to love sacrificially, able to communicate through language, able to laugh, etc. But none of them is as consistent a distinguishing feature as rationality. Note, first of all, that some of these are true of not just humans. "Social," for example, could also be said of all those animals that live in packs or groups, such as wolves, lions, bees,

---

[15] Note that Grotius agrees entirely with this point, as he says, in his *Rights of War and Peace*, "To this we must add, that these principles God has made more manifest by the laws which he has given, so that they may be understood by those whose minds have a feebler power of drawing inferences." Cf. *On the Rights of War*, xxvi.

[16] Aquinas, *On Being*, 31.

ants, etc. "Created in God's image," though attributed in the Bible to man alone is not offered as a proper definition of human beings, but, rather, as a description of their relationship to God.[17] In fact, the traditional understanding of this description has been that it was true of humans just because they are rational animals.[18] Secondly, some of these distinguishing features are better understood, not as properties which properly distinguish man from all other animals, but as properties which flow out of that feature which properly distinguishes man from all other animals. That is, the fact that man alone, of all the animals, is able to love sacrificially, communicate through language, laugh

---

[17] The term "relationship" can be somewhat ambiguous. By relationship here, we mean the fact that man is related to God as rational creation to rational creator. There will obviously be many consequences and implications of such a relationship.

[18] Some, such as Pietro Martyr Vermigli and John Walton argue that man is "created in the image of God" is because he has been given dominion over the world; cf. John Walton, *The Lost World of Genesis One: Ancient Cosmology and the Origins Debate* (Downers Grove, IL: InterVarsity Press, 2009), 67, 148. For Vermigli, however, this dominion is only made possible because man is a rational animal: "The beginning of Genesis teaches how man is the image of God.... This shows that the image of God consists in this, that he should rule over all creatures, as God is ruler over everything. Augustine often refers this to the memory, mind, and will, which as faculties of the same soul represent (as he said) the three persons in one substance. Yet this doctrine of Augustine rather shows the cause of the image. For man is not set above other creatures to have dominion over them for any other purpose than that he is endowed with reason, which reveals itself clearly by these three faculties." Cf. Peter Martyr Vermigli, *Philosophical Works: On the Relation of Philosophy to Theology*, trans. and ed. Joseph C. McLelland (Kirksville, MO: Sixteenth Century Essays & Studies, 1996), 42. Francis Turretin says that the image of God in man consists in three gifts given by God to man: (1) the rational nature of man, (2) the original righteousness of man, and (3) the dominion and immortality given by God to man. Cf. Francis Turretin, *Institutes of Elenctic Theology*, trans. George Musgrave Giger, ed. James T. Dennison, Jr. (Phillipsburg, NJ: P&R Publishing, 1992), 464-470.

(see the humour in a situation), and many other things, is due to the fact that man is a rational being. Humans are also able to voluntarily decide to put their own good aside for the good of another because they are rational. These distinguishing features of Human nature are what we should call essential attributes, that is, attributes which result from human nature. The word *rational* refers to, among other things, the capacity to reason, to consider abstract concepts for the sake of knowing, to deliberate about means to ends, etc. We propose, therefore, that humans are rational animals.

Human Ends and the Good

As we noted above, everything that exists has what we called a final cause—a reason for its existence, an end towards which it naturally tends. Not only does every being have a final cause, but the action of every animate being also has an end, or final cause. Crucially, we discover the end of each thing when we see that it habitually tends to direct itself towards a particular good.[19] Aquinas suggests this approach in his fifth way when he states, "We see that things which lack intelligence, such as natural bodies, act for an end, and this is evident from their acting always, or nearly always, in the same way, so as to obtain the best result."[20]

Though the final end of each being may be somewhat difficult to discern, it is often quite easy to discern the end of the individual actions of animate beings. We discover,

---

[19] Cf. John F. Wippel, *The Metaphysical Thought of Thomas Aquinas: From Finite Being to Uncreated Being* (Washington, D. C.: Catholic University of America Press, 2000), 480–81.

[20] Aquinas, *ST* I, Q. 2, A. 3, *Respondeo*.

for example, that the final end of an ear is to receive sound, and a good ear, an ear which successfully attains its end, is an ear which receives all those sounds which it is supposed to receive. We could say something similar about eyes and colour, the sense of touch and texture or shape, the nose and odors, and the tongue and flavour. Returning to our example of a fridge, we could say that the "nature" of a fridge is "a machine which preserves food by lowering the interior temperature of the machine." So, the end of a fridge is to preserve food by keeping it cold. Therefore, a good refrigerator is a fridge that successfully preserves food by the removal of warmth. A fridge which did not lower the temperature would be a terrible fridge! These judgments are objective judgments based upon the "nature" of the fridge. We see, then, that just as the formal cause of X is determined by its final cause, so also, we judge the proximity to X fully attaining to its formal cause by how close it comes to fully attaining its final cause. That is, X is said to be more or less good based upon how close it comes to attaining its natural end (that end which is proper to its nature).

These reflections allow us to propose a general definition of "the good." Aristotle proposes that

> If, then, there is some end of the things we do, which we desire for its own sake (everything else being desired for the sake of this), and if we do not choose everything for the sake of something else … clearly this must be the good and the chief good.[21]

---

[21] Aristotle, *Nicomachean Ethics*, book 1, 2, 1094a17-22, trans. W. D. Ross, ed. J. O. Urmson, in vol. 2 of *The Complete Works of Aristotle*, ed.

The general notion of good, then, is that the good is that which each thing desires for itself (and not for something else), and that end towards which each thing directs itself according to its nature. The end of each being is, therefore, its good, and each being is good in the measure that it obtains its good—that is, its end.[22]

It is worth noting, before continuing, that there are ends which humans choose for themselves—the ends of particular human actions—by which they approximate, more or less, to being truly human. Good human actions, considered as moral because they are the result of rational deliberation, would be no more than special cases of the general notion of the good.[23] We will give further consideration to good human actions in a moment, but it is also important to note that just as there are ends which humans choose for themselves, there is also an end which is natural to humans as humans—the ultimate end or final cause of human nature, God—who is the ultimate *telos* of all human

---

Jonathan Barnes, 2nd ed. (1984; repr., Princeton, NJ: Princeton University Press, 1995), 1729. Thomas Aquinas's comments on this point are helpful. He points out the reasoning behind this statement by noting, first of all, that "an end for the sake of which other ends are sought is of greater importance than they." Cf. Thomas Aquinas, *Commentary on Aristotle's* Nicomachean Ethics, lect. 2, 19, revised ed., trans. C. J. Litzinger (Notre Dame, IN: Dumb Ox Books, 1993), 7. Thomas Aquinas shows that there must be an ultimate end for if there were not, then there would be an infinite regress of ends leading to ends leading to ends, and no act would ever take place (Ibid., 7–8).

[22] Cf. Aristotle, *Nicomachean Ethics*, bk. 1, ch. 7, 1097a17–23. Note that this also allows the natural law theorist to easily escape the so called Naturalistic (Is/ought) fallacy, for goodness just is co-extensive with Being. Thus, insomuch as X is (insomuch as it attains to the full possession of its nature, or strays from it), x is good.

[23] Cf. Edward Feser, *Aquinas: Beginners Guides* (2009; repr., Oxford: Oneworld Publications, 2010), 176.

action, regardless of whether or not individual human beings are aware of it. Indeed, as many theologians have remarked, man was made to be united with God. Augustine, in his *Confessions*, said to God "Thou awakest us to delight in Thy praise; for Thou madest us for Thyself, and our heart is restless until it repose in Thee."[24] Aquinas says essentially the same thing: "Final and perfect happiness can consist in nothing else than the vision of the Divine Essence."[25] Or, in the words of the first question of the *Westminster Catechism*, "Man's chief end is to glorify God, and to enjoy him forever."[26] For man's ultimate good, and thus only source of ultimate and eternal happiness, is union with God.

Returning to our consideration of the good and human beings, we see, first of all, that as an animal, humans naturally pursue many natural ends like eating, growing, reproducing, etc. The human attempt to obtain nourishment, growth, and to reproduce is nothing more than the normal pursuit of the natural ends of an animal. There is, however, more to being a human than being an animal, for humans are rational animals. Indeed, that which distinguishes a human action from an animal action, that by which we judge a human action is or is not moral, is the question of whether or not the action accords with the rational aspect of human nature. Though human beings must, in order to be fully human, obtain ends proper to

---

[24] Augustine, *The Confessions*, in *Augustine*, vol. 18 of *Great Books of the Western World*, ed. Robert Maynard Hutchins, trans. Edward Bouverie Pusey (1952; repr., Chicago: Encyclopedia Britannica, 1988), 1.

[25] Aquinas, *ST* I-II, Q. 3, A. 8, *Respondeo*.

[26] Cf. Schaff, *The Evangelical Protestant Creeds*, 675, 676.

animals, because they are humans, they must obtain those ends in ways that are properly rational.

For example, put a hamburger in front of a normal dog and the dog will eat it—no second thoughts, no regrets, just satisfaction of the tendency towards nourishment. Put that same hamburger in front of a human, and the result will not be the same. Some humans, vegetarians, for example, will not eat the hamburger under almost any circumstances. They do not see hamburgers as "goods" to be pursued. Other humans, perhaps those on a dietary regime, might refuse to eat it because it has too many calories. They normally see the hamburger as a good to be pursued, but because of a self-imposed dietary regiment, they do not see it as a good to be pursued. Thus humans rationally deliberate about the ends they pursue, and about how they will pursue them. Edward Feser sums up quite well what we have been saying:

> Practical reason is directed by nature towards the pursuit of what the intellect perceives as good; what is *in fact* good is the realization or fulfillment of the various ends inherent in human nature; and thus a *rational* person will perceive this and, accordingly, direct his or her actions towards the realization or fulfillment of those ends. In this sense, good action is just that which is 'in accord with reason' (*ST* I-II.21.1; cf. *ST* I-II.90.1), and the moral skeptic's question 'Why should I do what is good?' has an obvious answer: because to be

rational *just is* (in part) to do what is good, to
fulfill the ends set for us by nature.[27]

This brings us to the question of the morality of an
action. Based upon what we have seen above, in order to
discern whether or not a particular action is moral or immoral, we must consider: (1) the nature and natural end of
the agent (for example, defecating in the neighbor's front
yard is immoral for a human being, but amoral for a dog);
(2) the end or purpose of the action (for example, to tell
the truth in order to malign another person's character is
immoral, but to tell the truth in order that justice be served
is morally good); (3) the motivations or intentions of the
action (for example, to tell the truth, in order that justice
be served, but motivated by the evil desire to get someone
out of the way of your own personal progress is immoral);
(4) the results or consequences of an action; (5) the means
by which the end was achieved; and (6) the circumstances
surrounding the action (the personal, social, political, and
religious contexts). Importantly, almost every one of these
elements, by which we determine the morality of an action,
is (a) teleological, and (b) related to either the nature of the
agent or the nature of the action.

We have shown, therefore, how we arrive at the conclusion that natures do exist and are instantiated in individuals of each species. We have also shown that a thing is
considered good in direct relation to the extent to which it
fully attains its proper end—the accomplishment of its
nature. From this it follows that we can, based upon our
knowledge of human nature, (1) discover normative laws
for all human beings—that is, that some actions are moral-

---

[27] Feser, *Aquinas*, 185.

ly good for human beings, that some actions are morally bad for human beings, and that the moral goodness of some actions depend upon the surrounding circumstances, motives, and means of the action in question; (2) make objective moral judgments concerning the relative goodness of individual human beings, in relationship to human nature (as we know it);[28] and (3) make moral judgments concerning the relative goodness of individual human actions in relation to the nature of the action and the natural end of that particular action. We propose, therefore, that we have successfully fulfilled the dual purpose of this section, showing how we arrive at the conclusion that there are essences or natures, and showing how the existence of these natures is foundational for natural law. We will now, in conclusion, consider the epistemological elements of natural law.

---

[28] It is important to note that only God—the artificer—knows precisely what human nature is supposed to be. Thus, when we discover what human nature is, even a small part of it, we are, quite literally, thinking God's thoughts after Him. The very fact that our knowledge of human nature is limited is one of the reasons why divine revelation in both inspired and inerrant scriptures, and in Christ himself, is important. The Word of God tells us what is wrong with humans and what humans are supposed to be like; then Christ comes and shows us just what humans are supposed to be and tells us that the only way to become like Him (to become truly human) is to put our faith in Him (Rom. 10:9–10, Eph. 2:8–10).

IV:
EPISTEMOLOGICAL ASPECTS OF NATURAL LAW

ONE OF THE necessary elements of a just law is that it is promulgated, it is made known to those to whom it applies. For example, typically, if you are not legally allowed to turn right at a red light, there will be a sign which informs you of this rule at each particular red light where that rule applies. This is not the case, however, on the Island of Montreal, for it is illegal on the entire island to turn right on a red light. So if you drive on the island of Montreal and you turn right on a red light, you risk getting a ticket. Complaining to the officer that you did not know about that law will not get you out of the ticket because you are legally responsible to obey the laws of the country you are in, even if you are not aware of those laws. This is a particular case of the well-known law principle known as *ignorantia juris non excusat* – ignorance of the law excuses not. Those who might complain about the "no turning on red lights" law on the island of Montreal actually have no excuse, for it is promulgated by way of large signs at each entrance to the island of Montreal.

What about natural law? Has it been "promulgated"? We have seen that it is founded upon (1) the divine creator, and (2) the divinely created essences, but can we know it? Is it not the case that no man can know the mind of God? For natural law to be true, humans must be able to arrive at some understanding of human morality *via* their own knowledge of human nature, limited though it is. The question, of course, is how do humans know human nature?

ABSTRACTION

Knowledge has this strange character of being *intentional.* This means it points to an object other than itself. In other words, all knowledge is *of* something; even the knowledge of the nature of knowledge is a knowledge *of* something. Étienne Gilson, in his important defense of methodical realism, states as much when he says of knowledge that "the first thing that it grasps, is a nature situated in an existence which is not that of the knower, the *ens* of a material nature."[1] Indeed, as Gilson later states, "the constant method of the scholastic is to go from things to concepts, in such a way that he needs many concepts to express the essence of one single thing."[2] The process of moving from the individual particular things to a concept which applies

---

[1] Étienne Gilson, *Le Réalisme Méthodique*, 2e ed. (Paris: Chez Pierre Téqui, 1937), 46. My translation. In French we read, « La première chose qu'il saisisse, c'est une nature posée dans une existence qui n'est pas la sienne, l'*ens* d'une nature matérielle. »

[2] Gilson, *Le Réalisme Méthodique*, 55. My translation. In French we read, « la méthode constante du scolastique est d'aller des choses aux concepts, de sorte qu'il lui faut plusieurs concepts pour exprimer l'essence d'une seule chose. »

to the many individuals is called, in Aristotelian-Thomistic philosophy, *abstraction*.

Knowledge, in Aristotelian-Thomistic philosophy, is explained through three degrees of abstraction, which is a word which portrays the notion of separation with the purpose of analysis. Oderberg notes that, for the Essentialist,

> Not only does all knowledge begin with the senses, but all immediate sensory perception is of particulars. It is from the particulars that we advance, through a process of abstraction, to the knowledge of universals, of which we form abstract concepts.[3]

Abstraction could be described as the act of concentrating one's attention on one part of a thing, without taking anything else, or other parts of that one thing, into account. For example, we concentrate our attention on this tree, rather than the whole forest; or, we notice quantity rather than color.

We can make two major distinctions in relationship to abstraction. First, we can make a distinction between what we call "abstraction of the whole" (*abstractio totalis*) and "abstraction of the part" (*abstractio formalis*). The *abstraction of the whole* is what a rational being does when it classifies the beings that present themselves to the person into general groups by the precise distinguishing features of the beings under consideration. For example, upon seeing Peter, John and James, we arrive at the general classification "man." Upon seeing a number of men, dogs, and

---

[3] Oderberg, *Real Essentialism*, 24.

horses we arrive at the general classification "animal." There is no precision in these classifications. As Maritain writes, "I am simply trying to reunite the common traits, to set up a simple notional framework common to such and such individuals."[4] Human beings begin engaging in abstraction of the whole very shortly after birth. It is through this first type of abstraction that we come to distinguish different genera and species.

The *abstraction of the form* (or of the part) is what happens when we separate the essence or nature of the being in question from its materiality. In this second order abstraction, we are no longer setting up general categories; we are instead trying to distinguish one essence from another, for example, the essence of human beings from the essence of horses or dogs. As Maritain states, "Here I am trying expressly to attain to the nature, the essence, the type of being, the locus of intelligible necessities."[5] It is within this second type of abstraction that we see the second major distinction: degrees of abstraction from matter. The three levels of abstraction are: (1) Abstraction from individual matter, (2) Abstraction from sensible matter, and (3) Abstraction from all matter. Aristotle used these three levels of abstraction as the basis for distinguishing between three general sciences: (1) Physics (which is divided up into (a) the natural sciences and (b) the philosophy of nature), (2) Mathematics, and (3) Metaphysics.

Through the two major types of abstraction (of the whole and of the part) we come to knowledge of the nature of whatever it is that we are considering. The more a

---

[4] Jacques Maritain, *Philosophy of Nature*, trans. Imelda C. Byrne (New York: The Philosophical Library, 1951), 19.

[5] Maritain, *Philosophy of Nature*, 19.

human being comes into contact with particular X's the more refined their understanding of the nature of X will become. This process of abstraction is what Oderberg is talking about when he says,

> As to observation of universals, we observe, say, greenness, by observing green things. When a medical researcher wants to study cancer, he does so by studying particular instances – organisms with cancer, or particular samples of cancerous growth in vitro, and so on. If you want to study human nature, you have to look at individual human beings. Although all *immediate* sensory experience is of particulars, we have indirect or *mediate* sensory experience of universals *by means of* our observation of particulars.[6]

We can, therefore, come to at least some knowledge of the natures of the things of this world, and, thus, to some knowledge of human nature.

THINKING GOD'S THOUGHTS AFTER HIM

Not only do human beings have knowledge of essences, such as human nature, through abstraction, but, when we arrive at knowledge of these essences, we are thinking Gods thoughts after Him. That is, the natures of the things that are known by human beings are known through observation of the particular existing instances of those essences. But, the particular existing instances of those essences are materialized individuals of that nature as it is

---

[6] Oderberg, *Real Essentialism*, 23–24.

known by God—materialized individuals of any one nature are simply instances of divine ideas (the exemplar
causes). This is illustrated in the following chart, in which
we portray the idea of man, in the mind of man, as founded upon his observation of the individual instances of man
in the created world. These individual instances in the
created world are, in turn, founded upon the divine idea of
human nature.[7]

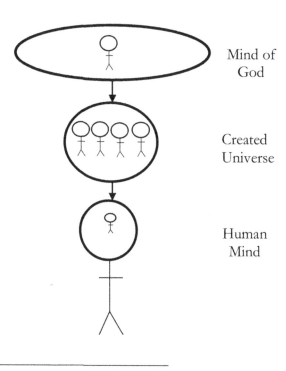

Mind of
God

Created
Universe

Human
Mind

---

[7] If there is a God who is the creative source of everything that exists in
the universe, then it is safe to assume that God created the universe
based upon His divine ideas. These ideas are then known by individual
humans through their observations of the created world. I would
suggest, therefore, that moderate realism is the logical consequence of
divine creation.

V:
SUMMARY CONCLUSION

WE SET out to discuss the philosophical foundations of natural law theory. We discovered, based upon the concept of natural law, that there were two metaphysical foundations of natural law: (1) the existence of a creator God, and (2) the existence of real natures. We also discovered that, along with these metaphysical principles, there was also an epistemological principle which is necessary for any coherent theory of natural law: (1) that the existing essences are, in principle, knowable by humans. We have shown why each of these philosophical principles is foundational for natural law theory, and how they work together to support the claim that there is an order or rule of human conduct which is (1) based upon human nature as created by God, (2) knowable by all men, through human intuition and reasoning (beginning from his observations of creation, in general; and human nature, in particular) alone, independent of any particular divine revelation provided through a divine spokesperson; and thus (3) normative for all human beings.

It should be noted that there is still much room for debate concerning just how natural law is known. For example, Jacques Maritain suggests that

> the judgments in which natural law is made manifest to practical Reason do not proceed from any conceptual, discursive, rational exercise of reason; they proceed from that *connaturality or congeniality* through which what is consonant with the essential inclinations of human nature is grasped by the intellect as good; what is dissonant, as bad.[1]

In other words, natural law is only known through intuitive knowledge, not through discursive knowledge. Some natural law theorists, following the rationalist and stoic philosophers such as Cicero, would probably disagree, saying that natural law, based upon reason, is known through discursive reasoning. Others, such as the authors of this book, take a mediating position whereby natural law is partially known intuitively, and partially known *via* discursive reasoning.[2] One could also discuss how sin and the Fall affect the human ability to know natural law. We will not be discussing these questions here, but in the rest of this guide we will seek to show that natural law is not only

---

[1] Maritain, *Natural Law*, 20.

[2] Such is the position of Aquinas, as he can be seen distinguishing between the primary or common precepts of natural law, which are self-evident, and the secondary or contingent precepts which are known through discursive reasoning (cf. Aquinas, *ST* I-II, Q. 94, A. 2, 4). Cf. David E. Luscombe, "Natural Morality and Natural Law," in *The Cambridge History of Later Medieval Philosophy*, ed. Norman Kretzmann, Anthony Kenny, and Jan Pinborg (1982; Cambridge: CUP, 2000), 711. Luscombe also points out that Francisco Suarez seems to hold a similar view of how humans come to know Natural Law (Ibid., 717).

philosophically coherent, and founded upon Being itself, but that natural law is also biblical.

PART II:

AN EXEGETICAL CASE FOR NATURAL LAW

VI. INTRODUCTION AND HYPOTHESES

THE BIBLE everywhere assumes, and in some places explicitly appeals to, natural law. The written book of God constantly bears witness to God's other book, the book of nature. To prove this, we will walk through Genesis to Revelation, noting some important sights along the way.

Apart from the question of natural law's biblical foundation and veracity, readers might wonder what the profit of pursuing this question could be. We will return to this query in the conclusion of the book, but there are in fact several ways recognizing natural law can help Christians, as will hopefully become evident throughout the rest of the argument: in apologetics, it helps us to demonstrate the goodness of God; in ethics, it provides Christian thinkers with clarity on subjects both addressed by Scripture and not; in history, it helps us to understand why post-apostolic Christians adhered to natural law from the outset of the church; in engagement with the world outside the church, it allows believers to recognize the goodness that has existed in the human race and its products throughout history; in law and politics, it provides a logical foundation for the unique kind of civilisation that Protestant Christianity produced; in exegesis, it clarifies the inner logic of the

New Testament's approach to the laws of the ⟨
Christian practice, it helps us to see the kind
believers have been called to.

MY HYPOTHESES

Given the conception of natural law which was presented
and defended in the previous section, the remainder of this
book will be to be used to show that Scripture presupposes this concept as reflecting reality. To be more specific, I
will attempt to prove the following propositions are supported by the Bible:

(N1) that there is an objective order to the universe
of the kind described above;

(N2) that this order is objectively visible, there to be
seen, whether one is wearing the spectacles of Scripture or
not;

(N3) that at least some unregenerate people perceive
this order.

One final comment, regarding the relation between
these hypotheses. The principles of justice suggest that if
N1 is true, the other two must be as well. That is, if God
has established an order that intrinsically binds people
morally, then he cannot hold them accountable for failures
to abide by it unless he also makes it known to them. For
the rest of this survey we will not focus on this logical
connection between the premises; its cogency, however,
adds strength to the argument as a whole.

VII:
THE HEBREW SCRIPTURES

THE WEALTH of evidence for natural law in Scripture surpasses my ability to catalogue it, at least in a reasonably brief period. What follows is only small sampling of what the Scriptures contain. It is however representative, and, by the end of the survey, I trust readers will be able to readily detect other evidence themselves.[1]

GENESIS

In the beginning, God created the heavens and the earth. At the end of the seventh day, he rested, having pronounced his work *good*. This is the first proclamation of the doctrine of natural law. Anything that would destroy or

---

[1] The work of John J. Collins in his *Encounters with Biblical Theology* (Minneapolis: Fortress Press, 2005), and Markus Bockmuehl in his *Jewish Law in Gentile Churches: Halakhah and the Beginning of Christian Public Ethics* (Grand Rapids: T & T Clark, 2003), are useful for study on this subject and I rely on them extensively in what follows. In the past, I have also consulted James Barr's book *Biblical Faith and Natural Theology: The Gifford Lectures for 1991: Delivered in the University of Edinburgh* (Oxford: OUP, 2000).

corrupt this good created order, logic would dictate, would be bad or evil.[2]

Genesis 2 gives us another piece of evidence. God saw lonely Adam, and said this was "not good" (Gen. 2:18). What could this statement mean? It must communicate something like, "Given the nature of Adam, given his intrinsic properties, his remaining without a complement-woman will harm him." God evaluated the kind of being Adam was and judged he was not in a good situation. Adam's male form was intrinsically directed toward a female companion that he lacked and needed for his fulfillment.

So already, after the first two chapters of the Bible, we see an affirmation of an objective order (N1), a natural law.

EXODUS

Bockmuehl[3] mentions the case of Jethro in Exodus 18. During his visit with Moses, Jethro noticed people bringing cases to judge consumed all of the prophet's time. He responded: "What you are doing is not good.... For the thing is too heavy for you. You are not able to do it alone" (vs. 17-18).[4] Jethro's basic criticism was that Moses was failing to steward his time: in this regard, his actions were

---

[2] The possibility of violating this created order does not contradict an Augustinian, Thomist, or Calvinist view of providence and grace, of course. The kind of freedom human beings have is freedom to violate what Thomists would call the antecedent will, or the Reformed the revealed will, of God, not his consequent or secret will. The natural law is the revelation of God's moral will, and it is no violation of Augustine, Thomas, and Calvin's doctrine to say this will can be resisted.

[3] Bockmuehl, *Jewish Law*, 91.

[4] This and all following biblical quotations come from the English Standard Version.

"not good." Here we have an example of someone outside of the visible assembly of God's people (though most likely a God-fearer of some kind), who offers moral wisdom to God's lawgiver himself, Moses. Jethro's suggestion could not have been derived from the Torah, or else he would not have needed to give it. His advice is simple common sense. Moses needed to delegate and divide the labour; his time and energy simply could not handle the workload. And he was certainly able to delegate. Jethro perceived the problem and solution where no explicit divine law addressed the issue. Now of course, one could say that Jethro's advice is derived by extension from some more basic Mosaic principle, but just as obviously, this advice is common sense. [5] It surely strains credulity to suggest that only someone who had read Moses' law could come up with this suggestion. And yet it obviously benefitted Moses, and so fulfilled the natural law, which points people toward their own good. This example thus conforms to N1, and probably suggests N2. If Jethro was unregenerate, it proves N3.

DEUTERONOMY

Collins highlights[6] Deuteronomy 4:5-6, where God tells Moses:

---

[5] As G. A. Chadwick notes, "From the whole of this narrative we see clearly that the intervention of God for Israel is no more to be regarded as superseding the exercise of human prudence and common-sense, than as dispensing with valour in the repulse of Amalek, and with patience in journeying through the wilderness." See *The Book of Exodus* (London: Hodder and Stoughton, 1898), 263. Cf. Herman J. Keyser, *A Commentary on Exodus* (Grand Rapids, MI: Zondervan, 1940), 256–57. Keyser notes that Jethro's advice was a fruit of his "eastern wisdom."

[6] Collins, *Encounters*, 101–2.

See, I have taught you statutes and rules, as the Lord my God commanded me, that you should do them in the land that you are entering to take possession of it. Keep them and do them, for that will be your wisdom and your understanding in the sight of the peoples, who, when they hear all these statutes, will say, 'Surely this great nation is a wise and understanding people.'

If Israel keeps the law, God says the nations will conclude it is a wise and understanding people. What is the logic of this promise? It must be that the nations will look on and see how obeying this law leads to flourishing, to human good. But this assumes several things. Firstly, it assumes there is an objective human good. The contrary assertion would be that good is whatever the law says it is and nothing more. But then, the peoples' statement would mean nothing more than: "Surely this is a nation that lives according to its laws." Obviously, this is nonsense. Rather, it must assume, secondly, that the pagans know what human flourishing is, and that they can see that obeying God's law leads to it. This certainly proves N1. It may even prove N3, unless we assume only regenerate Gentiles draw this conclusion from their observations.

ISAIAH

Bockmuehl highlights the polemic against the nonsense of idolatry in Isaiah.[7] Chapter 44 contains a detailed description of the folly of this practice, beginning with a narration

---

[7] Bockmuehl, *Jewish Law*, 92.

of how idol makers painstakingly gather materials and skilfully design their idols, while using the same materials to cook their dinner. Verse 19 is a good summary of Isaiah's reaction:

> No one considers, nor is there knowledge or discernment to say, "Half of it I burned in the fire; I also baked bread on its coals; I roasted meat and have eaten. And shall I make the rest of it an abomination? Shall I fall down before a block of wood?"

At first it may seem like 19 contradicts N3, but this need not be the case. Romans 1 alone suggests there can be a kind of simultaneously knowing-and-not-knowing (as we shall see when we get to that text), or at least knowledge-preceding-culpable-ignorance, and no doubt the same understanding is operating here.[8] Isaiah makes an observation about pagan behaviour: they clearly, in some way, do not see the insanity of what they are doing, or else they would stop doing it. Yet, it is still *insanity*, action that defies reality, which at minimum proves N1. Further, that Isaiah describes this not as mere ignorance, but rather as delusion,[9] proves N2: the sheer facts of the nature of

---

[8] Indeed, John N. Oswalt, in his NICNT commentary on Isaiah, also notes this parallel with Romans 1, noting that "The solution has always been, even for one so concerned to uphold divine sovereignty as Calvin, to maintain that this covering over was not arbitrary, but in response to the freely chosen acts of the idolaters. In this, Calvin and all the rest of us are following the lines laid out by Paul in Rom. 1." See *The Book of Isaiah: Chapters 40-66*, NICNT (Grand Rapids, MI: Wm. B. Eerdmans Publishing, 1998), 185.

[9] Oswalt calls this a "self-delusion", which brings out just how insane the idol worshippers really are (*The Book of Isaiah*, 186.). Edward J. Young, in his classic commentary on Isaiah, brings out just how

wood and of divinity prove that they cannot be identical. This is not a truth that could be known only by means of historical testimony about the events of, e.g., the Exodus. It is rather something obvious on its face. The tone of derision throughout the text seems to imply N3, as well, that though pagans are blind in a sense, they are culpably blind. They have ignored reality and for that reason have ceased to see it.[10]

JEREMIAH AND AMOS

Jeremiah 8:7 draws a parallel between what we are calling natural law, and the special revelation of Scripture:[11]

> Even the stork in the heavens
> knows her times,
> and the turtledove, swallow, and crane
> keep the time of their coming,
> but my people know not
> the rules of the Lord.

---

deluded idol worshippers are when he states that "The phrase is stronger and more forceful than the ordinary 'to place upon the heart'; it suggests that the one who meditates has control of his thought. If he did actually permit himself to know what he was doing and to perceive its true significance he would realize his folly and abandon it." See *The Book of Isaiah* (1972; repr., Grand Rapids: Wm. B. Eerdmans Publishing, 1979), 3:181. Cf. J. Alec Motyer, *The Prophecy of Isaiah: An Introduction & Commentary* (Downers' Grove, IL: InterVarsity Press, 1993), 346-347.

[10] It should also be noted that divinely inspired authors are not the only authors to ridicule the insanity of idol worship. Many unregenerate classical authors, such as Horace, point out the insanity of worshipping an idol, in much the same way as Isaiah (cf. Motyer, *The Prophecy*, 346.).

[11] Cf. John Bright, *Jeremiah: Introduction, Translation, and Notes* (Garden City, NY: Doubleday, 1965), 63.

The lower animals follow natural law, and so we have a witness here to (N1), though in this case the prophet does not highlight the ethical aspect of the natural order.

Bockmuehl notes a similar passage in Amos 6:12: [12]

> Do horses run on rocks?
> Does one plow there with oxen?
> But you have turned justice into poison
> and the fruit of righteousness into wormwood—

In this case, the plowing analogy provides an example of drawing an ethical inference from the natural order: rocky ground is of such a nature that trying to plow in it, when better land is available, would be senseless. Senselessness, of course, is another way of speaking of foolishness, which is the name the Bible gives to actions which attempt to defy the good and wise order intrinsic to creation. And wasting one's time and energy in such an agricultural endeavor would surely exemplify foolishness. So this brief analogy assumes N1 and N2. Further, the analogy present in the text probably assumes an unregenerate person could see the foolishness of such an act. The immediate parallel is an act so foolish a horse has the sense not to do it; clearly, this is not the kind of behaviour for which regeneration is necessary to recognize as foolish. Thus Amos seems to support N3 as well.

JOB

Bockmuehl also refers to an important example of natural law ethics in practice.[13] Job (31:13-15) says during his final appeal:

---

12 Bockmuehl, *Jewish Law*, 92.

If I have rejected the cause of my manservant or my
maidservant,
when they brought a complaint against me,
what then shall I do when God rises up?
When he makes inquiry, what shall I answer him?
Did not he who made me in the womb make him?
And did not one fashion us in the womb?

Job affirms N1 at minimum in this case. More specifically, he highlights an aspect of the created order, and
expects his interlocutors to see that this "is" has an obvious "ought" implied in it. The common human nature
shared between Job and his slave, given to them both by
their common Lord, requires Job treat him with equity.
The force of his argument as it stands in the text depends
entirely on this observable common humanity.

A part of the Lord's response to Job also serves our
purposes here: when God gives Job his answer, he directs
the righteous man back to aspects of the created order,
and expects him to infer the proper perspective about the
Creator from that order.[14] More specifically, God reminds
Job of his ignorance about how the Lord governs the universe. Job gets the point (Job 40:3-5; 42:1-6). So this text
assumes, again, at least N1, if not N2 and N3.

And indeed, Job had already derived this lesson from
nature earlier in the book. Collins notes a part of Job's
argument that anticipates a perspective of Proverbs, when
he declares that Wisdom relates to the order of creation.
Job 28:20-28 says:

---

[13] Bockmuehl, *Jewish Law*, 94-95.

[14] Collins, *Encounters*, 96.

From where, then, does wisdom come?
And where is the place of understanding?
It is hidden from the eyes of all living
and concealed from the birds of the air.
Abaddon and Death say,
'We have heard a rumor of it with our ears.'
"God understands the way to it,
and he knows its place.
For he looks to the ends of the earth
and sees everything under the heavens.
When he gave to the wind its weight
and apportioned the waters by measure,
when he made a decree for the rain
and a way for the lightning of the thunder,
then he saw it and declared it;
he established it, and searched it out.
And he said to man,
'Behold, the fear of the Lord, that is wisdom,
and to turn away from evil is understanding.'"

We cannot overlook the connection between 20-27 and 28. One commentator writes:

> Having shown God as the Source of wisdom,
> the author now makes his application to man.
> Man must look to God for wisdom. Man may
> share in it only through a knowledge of the
> revealed mind of God. To acknowledge him
> as God and live within the sphere of his life-

giving precepts is wisdom for man (Deut. 4:5–6; Ps. 111:10; Prov. 8:4–9; 9:10).[15]

Once again, the objective structure of the universe has ethical implications (N1). The fact that man lacks wisdom, but that God undoubtedly possesses it (something clear from reflection upon creation), means that man must go to God for that wisdom. In other words, natural law requires worship of the Creator.

PSALMS

The obvious place to go for natural law in the Psalms is Psalm 19.[16] Because this text is one of the central Old Testament passages on this topic, we will look at it in its entirety:

> [1] The heavens declare the glory of God,
> and the sky above proclaims his handiwork.
> [2] Day to day pours out speech,
> and night to night reveals knowledge.
> [3] There is no speech, nor are there words,
> whose voice is not heard.
> [4] Their voice goes out through all the earth,
> and their words to the end of the world.
> In them he has set a tent for the sun,

---

[15] Elmer B. Smick, "Job," in *The Expositor's Bible Commentary: 1 & 2 Kings, 2 & 2 Chronicles, Ezra, Nehemiah, Esther, Job*, ed. Frank E. Gaebelein (Grand Rapids: Zondervan Publishing House, 1988), 977.

[16] Derek Kidner, for example, notes both that this Psalm speaks quite clearly of both General and Special Revelation, and that this Psalm may be foundational to Paul's reference to what the created universe tells us of God, in Romans 1:18-19. Cf. Derek Kidner, *Psalms 1-72: An Introduction and Commentary* (Downers' Grove, IL: InterVarsity Press, 1973), 97.

5 which comes out like a bridegroom leaving his chamber,

and, like a strong man, runs its course with joy.

6 Its rising is from the end of the heavens,

and its circuit to the end of them,

and there is nothing hidden from its heat.

7 The law of the Lord is perfect,

reviving the soul;

the testimony of the Lord is sure,

making wise the simple;

8 the precepts of the Lord are right,

rejoicing the heart;

the commandment of the Lord is pure,

enlightening the eyes;

9 the fear of the Lord is clean,

enduring forever;

the rules of the Lord are true,

and righteous altogether.

10 More to be desired are they than gold,

even much fine gold;

sweeter also than honey

and drippings of the honeycomb.

11 Moreover, by them is your servant warned;

in keeping them there is great reward.

12 Who can discern his errors?

Declare me innocent from hidden faults.

13 Keep back your servant also from presumptuous sins;

let them not have dominion over me!

Then I shall be blameless,

and innocent of great transgression.

> [14] Let the words of my mouth and the meditation of
> my heart
> be acceptable in your sight,
> O Lord, my rock and my redeemer.

Many commentators have noted the parallel between verses 1-6 and 7-14 (beginning with, "The law of the Lord"), but I want to emphasize the connection of this text to both Genesis 1, and to natural law. In verses 1-6 we are treated to an admiration of the goodness of the heavens. As they stand, they declare their Maker's glory. In the beginning, after God had created the stars and the sun, and had given them their ongoing functions to perform, he concluded that it was good (Gen. 1:18). David agrees here: when the sun (representative of the whole heavens, no doubt) runs its daily circuit, it obey its Maker's law with joy (Ps. 19:5). The heavens do what they were made to do, and that is what it means for them to flourish, and so they are "happy."

The second half of the Psalm draws the readers back to the human realm, and says, essentially: human beings likewise flourish when they live as they were always intended to live. And this path is marked out for them by the Torah.

But note: if there were no objective human goodness, a fact that existed alongside the Torah, not simply reduced to it, the declarations of verses 7-8 would have no meaning. They would simply utter tautologies: "the law of the Lord is perfect, making the soul conform to the law of the Lord." But the Psalmist of course means more than this: he means that obedience to God's written law achieves human flourishing, something which is ultimately determined by the way God made human beings.

Thus Psalm 19 affirms N1. It also, by saying that the orderliness of the heavenly bodies declares God's glory, affirms N2.

PROVERBS

The book of Proverbs provides an abundance of support for the Christian doctrine of natural law. It continually asserts that the foundation of wisdom in creation comes from its Creator, who founded the universe with wisdom (Prov. 3:9; 8:22-31).[17] This, as we noted earlier, eliminates any possibility of natural law being "autonomous" or "independent," and the best representatives of the tradition, like Aquinas, have always agreed with Scripture on this matter.

Yet, the pervasive presence of wisdom in creation, a presence explained by the Creator's use of it, means that wisdom speaks with its own voice in all places (Prov. 8:1-11). Wisdom is not found solely in the synagogue in the pages of Torah; it calls out in the streets and in the markets.[18] This point is just as important as the dependence of natural law on God. For we Christians are not monists: we really do believe that beings other than God exist. Consequently, we also believe the wisdom inherent in all creatures can speak to us, just as much as God can directly intervene in the course of history to speak to us. However, none of this implies that creatures somehow exist apart from God's continual sustaining. Rather, as Aquinas notes, the opposite is the case. Their continued existence makes

---

[17] Collins, *Encounters*, 100.

[18] The contrast with the pages of Torah in the synagogue is mine, but cf. Collins, *Encounters*, 96.

no sense apart from a necessary being who keeps them from falling into annihilation.

Collins elaborates on two fundamental concepts in Proverbial wisdom which help to give detail to what Scripture says natural law teaches. First, wisdom teaches "limit." That is, it teaches humanity's control over history is never comprehensive (e.g., Prov. 27.1).[19] This demands humility and ethical behaviour, for human beings are never totally in control (Prov. 21:30; 19:31; 16:1; Prov. 3:7).[20] Second, wisdom teaches "order." One of the fundamental aspects of this order is what could be called the "act and consequence" structure of reality. As Collins puts it, "There is no doubt that the insight that certain acts (or attitudes) have necessary consequences is fundamental to proverbial thinking from the earliest times."[21] There is, as Francis Schaeffer might say, "real reality." Indeed, Proverbs often contain explicit observations about the normal course of life, which provide the reason for their counsel: e.g., Prov. 27:23-24.[22]

In Proverbs the wise man becomes wise by observing. The fool, on the other hand, is the man who does not observe; he "despise[s] wisdom" (Prov. 1:7). It is important we recognize this fact, for it tells us something about the character of natural law. It is obvious that Proverbs supports N1 and N2, but it also, by its condemnation of the fool supports N3. The fool is not the one who remains ignorant of wisdom because he is outside the visible

---

[19] Collins, *Encounters*, 97.

[20] Collins, *Encounters*, 97.

[21] Collins, *Encounters*, 99,

[22] Collins, *Encounters*, 107.

church. Rather, he is the one who has refused to learn what he could have learned from observing the world, if it were not for his corrupted and hard heart. Christianity does not say humanity is condemned solely because it defies God's specially revealed positive laws, though of course it does say people who have defied such laws stand condemned. Adam, all the Israelites, all Christians, and everyone who has heard their testimony, have been in this position. But Proverbs, and the Scriptures more generally, also say God condemns the human race because humanity has actively and intentionally spurned the moral order that constantly surrounds it, and which "calls out in the streets."

ECCLESIASTES

Another important text for the biblical presentation of natural law appears in the Preacher's book, more specifically in the famous passage of 3:1-8:

> For everything there is a season, and a time for every matter under heaven:
> a time to be born, and a time to die;
> time to plant, and a time to pluck up what is planted;
> a time to kill, and a time to heal;
> a time to break down, and a time to build up;
> a time to weep, and a time to laugh;
> a time to mourn, and a time to dance;
> a time to cast away stones, and a time to gather stones together;
> a time to embrace, and a time to refrain from embracing;

a time to seek, and a time to lose;
a time to keep, and a time to cast away;
a time to tear, and a time to sew;
a time to keep silence, and a time to speak;
a time to love, and a time to hate;
a time for war, and a time for peace.

Dr. Collins refers to this famed speech because it presents the limits of the 'rules' we find in Proverbs, and it certainly does provide a big-picture context for the practical application of those norms. As Dr. Collins says, "Since proverbs are not universally valid laws but admit of exceptions, their applicability depends on the identification of the right time."[23] However, to imagine this is a correction of natural law thinking would be mistaken. The idea that natural law leaves open particular decisions to the work of prudence or discernment has been recognized throughout history. To return to an exemplary advocate, Aquinas speaks about this aspect of law in his discussion of human law.

First, in *ST* I-II, Q. 95, A.2, Thomas explains that a law can be derived from natural law in two ways: first as a deductive entailment, but also second as a particularization of a general rule. He gives an analogy here of a craftsmen looking to build a house, who must therefore build one type of house and not another, and an example in polities' decisions how to punish violations of natural law, which punishments are not specified in nature itself.[24]

Second, he makes other important observations about the application of natural law in the following Ques-

---

[23] Collins, *Encounters*, 114.

[24] Aquinas *ST* I-II, Q. 95, A. 2, *respondeo*.

tion. In the course of discussing Isidore's description of the nature of law (with which he agrees), he recounts that one characteristic of it is that it must be helpful to discipline. Elaborating on this, he explains that for Isidore, law must be just, possible to nature, according to the customs of the country, and adapted to place and time. These criteria mean that law must be according to reason, take into account the ability of nature, be in accord with social custom (as society is necessary to human life), and fitting for its precise circumstances.[25]

Natural law, then, leaves open some decisions to human determination, and these judgments are wisely made when they accord with "place and time," much as the Preacher says. True wisdom does not desire merely positive laws, but understands the need for a certain measure of subjectivity when it comes to the particulars.

---

[25] Aquinas *ST* I-II, Q. 95, A. 3, *respondeo*.

VIII:
EXTRACANONICAL JEWISH LITERATURE

JEWISH extracanonical literature, including but not limited to the Apocrypha, provides the context and background that formed the mental furniture of the first hearers of the NT. It also provides the earliest example of how the OT was interpreted with regards to our subject matter. As long as we allow the Scriptures to push back against this context if and when it wishes, we cannot be harmed by knowing more about it. And indeed, we will see, the NT largely agrees with the perspective we will survey here.

BEN SIRACH

Sirach begins to praise the glory of the Creator in his works with this comment (42:15–16):

> Now will I recall God's works;
> what I have seen, I will repeat.
> Through the Lord's word came his works;
> he accepts the one who does his will.
> As the shining sun is clear to all,

so the glory of the Lord fills his works;[1]

Bockmuehl rightly identifies this speech (he refers to the entirety of 42:15–43:33) as an example of natural theology.[2] The point of 42:16 is obvious enough: the clarity of the Sun's light to all people is an appropriate analogy to the glory of God which all people can see in all God's works. Of course, the idea of God's glory 'clearly' apparent in creation is not a "value neutral" description. Manifest glory demands appropriate response, and so this text affirms N1, N2, and N3 in the space of two verses.

TESTAMENT OF NAPHTALI

The Testament of Naphtali, part of the highly controverted apocryphal Testaments of the Twelve Patriarchs,[3] a book which claims to offer the dying commands of the sons of Jacob, provides an even clearer example of natural law thinking. Bockmuehl points to 3:2–5:[4]

Sun, moon, and stars do not alter their order; thus you should not alter the law of God by

---

[1] Patrick W. Skehan and Alexander A. Di Lella, O.F.M., vol. 39, *The Wisdom of Ben Sira: A New Translation With Notes, Introduction and Commentary*, Anchor Yale Bible (New Haven; London: Yale University Press, 2008), 484.

[2] Bockmuehl, *Jewish Law*, 98.

[3] This work may not strictly conform to the limits of this chapter, as some scholars argue it is a Christian work, while others argue elements were only interpolated by Christians. Academic editions and commentaries on the text will provide further discussion on the origins of the text for interested readers; probably it was written sometime after the destruction of Jerusalem, and certainly before Tertullian, who cites it.

[4] Bockmuehl, *Jewish Law*, 101.

the disorder of your actions. The gentiles, because they wandered astray and forsook the Lord, have changed the order, and have devoted themselves to stones and sticks, patterning themselves after wandering spirits. But you, my children, shall not be like that: In the firmament, in the earth, and in the sea, in all the products of his workmanship discern the Lord who made all things, so that you do not become like Sodom, which departed from the order of nature. Likewise the Watchers departed from nature's order; the Lord pronounced a curse on them at the Flood. On their account he ordered that the earth be without dweller or produce.[5]

Naphtali's logic runs as follows: the heavens follow God's order, and thus do rightly. Therefore, you also ought to follow God's order. The Gentiles forsook the Lord, and began to worship created things, and thereby have "changed" God's order. In contrast, the children of Naphtali must do the opposite: in the created order, they ought to discern God as the Creator (and, implicitly, worship that Creator, and not what they discern to be his creatures). The patriarch then gives two more examples from Genesis of figures who violated "the order of nature": Sodom, and the Watchers, reflecting the common interpretation that "the Sons of God" who married "the daughters of men" in Genesis 6 were fallen angels intermarrying with

---

[5] James H. Charlesworth, *The Old Testament Pseudepigrapha, Volume 1: Apocalyptic Literature and Testaments* (New York; London: Yale University Press, 1983), 812.

humans. This would be a type of inter-species mating, obviously contrary to nature. What is manifest through this whole text is that nature itself is God's order, and therefore violation of it means, *ipso facto*, violation of God's will. The text obviously proves N1 and N2, and by describing the Gentiles as wicked in the very next line of the book,[6] it confirms what should be obvious from this paragraph alone: the Gentiles, inhabitants of Sodom, and Watchers are culpable for violating the order of nature. Thus N3 is proven by implication, for absolute ignorance is exculpatory.

PSEUDO-PHOCYLIDES

Bockmuehl also rightly calls attention to the pseudepigraphal Jewish wisdom text of *Pseudo-Phocylides*,[7] which contains comments such as:

> [175] Do not remain unmarried, lest you die nameless.
> [176] Give nature her due, you also, beget in your turn as you were begotten.[8]

---

[6] "These things I say, my children, for I have read in the holy writing of Enoch that ye yourselves also will depart from the Lord, walking according to all wickedness of the Gentiles, and ye will do according to all the iniquity of Sodom."

[7] Bockmuehl, *Jewish Law*, 102. This text was probably written somewhere between 100 BC and AD 100, shedding light on the context of the New Testament.

[8] James H. Charlesworth, *The Old Testament Pseudepigrapha and the New Testament, Volume 2: Expansions of the "Old Testament" and Legends, Wisdom, and Philosophical Literature, Prayers, Psalms and Odes, Fragments of Lost Judeo-Hellenistic Works* (New Haven; London: Yale University Press, 1985), 580.

...[190] Do not transgress with unlawful sex the limits set by nature.

[191] For even animals are not pleased by intercourse of male with male.[9]

These sentences affirm N1 and N2, and the latter, by arguing that even animals recognize natural law, supports N3.

WISDOM OF SOLOMON

The three most famous Jewish sources supporting natural law, however, are the *Wisdom of Solomon*, Philo, and Josephus. *Wisdom*, scholars have concluded, rather than engaging simply with Platonism and Stoicism, assumes a background of Middle Platonism and Middle Stoicism, both of which more closely approximated the Jewish cosmology of a transcendent Creator alongside an intermediate order.[10] It is also worth noting that many scholars have seen *Wisdom* in particular behind Paul's logic in Romans 1, which may be possible (if Paul knew pagan poets, he could have known *Wisdom*). In *Wisdom* 13:1–9 we hear words such as these:

> For all men who were ignorant of God were foolish by nature;
> and they were unable from the good things that are seen to know him who exists,
> nor did they recognize the craftsman while

---

[9] James H. Charlesworth, *The Old Testament Pseudepigrapha and the New Testament, Volume 2: Expansions of the "Old Testament" and Legends, Wisdom, and Philosophical Literature, Prayers, Psalms and Odes, Fragments of Lost Judeo-Hellenistic Works* (New Haven: Yale University Press, 1985), 581.

[10] Collins, *Encounters*, 119.

paying heed to his works;

but they supposed that either fire or wind or swift air,

or the circle of the stars, or turbulent water,

or the luminaries of heaven were the gods that rule the world.

If through delight in the beauty of these things men assumed them to be gods,

let them know how much better than these is their Lord,

for the author of beauty created them.

And if men were amazed at their power and working,

let them perceive from them

how much more powerful is he who formed them.

For from the greatness and beauty of created things comes a corresponding perception of their Creator.

Yet these men are little to be blamed,

for perhaps they go astray

while seeking God and desiring to find him.

For as they live among his works they keep searching,

and they trust in what they see, because the things that are seen are beautiful.

Yet again, not even they are to be excused;

for if they had the power to know so much that they could investigate the world,

how did they fail to find sooner the Lord of these things?

The author of Wisdom undeniably affirmed N1 and N2; the logic of this passage implies something like N3, in that even unregenerate pagans are blamed for failing to respond to what was visible.

PHILO

That Philo supported the doctrine this essay is defending will surprise no one. I will provide just one clear example in the text of *The Life of Moses* 2.48:

> ...for he was not like any ordinary compiler of history, studying to leave behind him records of ancient transactions as memorials to future ages for the mere sake of affording pleasure without any advantage; but he traced back the most ancient events from the beginning of the world, commencing with the creation of the universe, in order to make known two most necessary principles. First, that the same being was the father and creator of the world, and likewise the lawgiver of truth; secondly, that the man who adhered to these laws, and clung closely to a connection with and obedience to nature, would live in a manner corresponding to the arrangement of the universe with a perfect harmony and union, between his words and his actions and between his actions and his words.[11]

---

[11] Charles Duke Yonge, trans., *The Works of Philo: Complete and Unabridged* (Peabody, MA: Hendrickson, 1995), 495.

JOSEPHUS

The great Jewish historian concurs, too, with our position. A few quotes from one section, *Against Apion* 2.190-219, provide the clearest examples:

> What are the things then that we are commanded or forbidden?—They are simply and easily known. The first command is concerning God, and affirms that God contains all things, and is a being every way perfect and happy, self-sufficient, and supplying all other beings; the beginning, the middle, and the end of all things. He is manifest in his works and benefits, and more conspicuous than any other being whatsoever, but as to his form and magnitude, he is most obscure.[12]

And a little later:

> But then, what are our laws about marriage? That law owns no other mixture of sexes but that which nature hath appointed, of a man with his wife, and that this be used only for the procreation of children. But it abhors the mixture of a male with a male.[13]

---

[12] William Whiston, trans., *The Works of Josephus: Complete and Unabridged* (Peabody: Hendrickson, 1987).

[13] Whiston, trans., *The Works of Josephus: Complete and Unabridged* (Peabody: Hendrickson, 1987).

1Q27 1.i.9-11 AND THE RABBIS

On the other hand, according to Bockmuehl, two groups of Jews show little concern with natural law: the compilers of the Qumran scrolls, and the Rabbis. In the case of the former, Bockmuehl does provide one example of a kind of natural law reasoning, in 1Q27:[14]

> It is true that all the peoples reject evil, yet it advances in all of them. It is true that truth is esteemed in the utterances of all the nations – yet is there any tongue or language that grasp it? What nation wants to be oppressed by another that is stronger? Or who wants his money to be stolen by a wicked man? Yet what nation is there that has not oppressed its neighbor? Where is the people that has not robbed the wealth of another…?

In fact, this is more clearly a witness to what was classically known as "the law of the nations" (*ius gentium*), which is the set of legal customs commonly held by all human societies. However, it may assume some awareness of the "obvious" reason for these jurisprudential commonplaces, e.g., pain is self-evidently not desirable, and so no nation wants to be oppressed. Regardless, the Qumran writers recognize that when people break these laws, they do so not out of total ignorance of the good, but rather in defiance of their knowledge.

Before moving on to the NT data, it is worth considering what the significance is of the departure of these two groups from the pattern we see elsewhere. At this point, it

---

[14] Bockmuehl, *Jewish Law*, 104.

may be relevant that, as Dr. James B. Jordan has noted in one place:

> Jesus bluntly accused the Jews of His day of not understanding the Mosaic revelation, because they had reduced it to mere law (Mark 7:1-23). He stated that the first purpose of the Torah was to reveal God, and thus to reveal Him as the Son of God. Had the Jews been reading the Torah properly, they would have recognized Jesus as God (John 5:45-46). The fact that they did not recognize Him meant that they were misreading Moses (Luke 24:27).
>
> How does the Torah point to God? Symbolically. Everything created by God reveals Him, and thus is a symbol of Him in some particular as well as general sense. The same is true of every aspect of the Bible. The Old Covenant is a type of the New, and everything in it symbolizes and points to God and Christ. Everything in the "Mosaic law" points to God, and typifies the Christ to come. It is this symbolic dimension that is primary, because it is the symbolic dimension that reveals God's person and plan.
>
> We have to say, then, that the reason the Jews did not recognize Jesus as the fulfillment of the Mosaic revelation is because they had

abandoned the symbolic approach to the Torah. They had reduced it to mere law.[15]

Is it possible that, just as the Rabbis misread the Torah, overlooking its symbolic figuration of Christ, so they
might have missed the significance, or at least importance
of, the way nature signifies God and the meaning of human life, because of the same spiritual problem? To put it
a different way: the Rabbis and Pharisees missed that Jesus
was the fulfillment of the law because they were determined to understand the Jewish Torah as an end in itself.
They were blinded to the end at which the Torah was
pointed, and so in fact misunderstood the meaning of the
law. But this same psychological failure, this determination
to see the law as an end in itself, and to secure a unique
importance for Torah as itself the foundation of the cosmos, could also blind them to the existence and importance of natural law. Indeed, the result of seeing the
law as an end in itself was a failure to obey the weightier
things of the law, such as mercy, justice, and faithfulness.
The aims which embody the flourishing of human beings
were the very things occluded by the Pharisaical approach
to the law's purpose; and it is those weightier things of the
Torah that natural law also most clearly communicates to
human beings.

The law of nature cannot provide grounds for any
one section of humanity to focus on its special characteristics, for by its very essence all people possess the natural

---

[15] James B. Jordan, *Studies in Food and Faith*, 43 (digital version). Jordan
has arguably described natural law in yet another way: symbols are
communicative realities. To say that every created thing symbolizes God
is to say that all things, in their intrinsic structure, are intended to make
God known to those who observe those things.

law. It was thus of no use to, and perhaps could even threaten, the major concerns of the successors of the Pharisees. But the same characteristics of the natural law make it *a priori* likely that a catholic religion like Christianity would have some use for it. And, as we shall see in the next instalment, this *a priori* was realized *a posteriori*.

IX:
THE CHRISTIAN SCRIPTURES

AS WE shall see, the teaching of the New Testament on natural law stands in continuity with the Old Testament and most extracanonical Jewish literature.

JESUS

The teaching of our Lord provides several examples of natural law reasoning. Most of them, in fact, are among his most memorable sayings. For example (in Matt 6:25–26):

> Therefore I tell you, do not be anxious about your life, what you will eat or what you will drink, nor about your body, what you will put on. Is not life more than food, and the body more than clothing? Look at the birds of the air: they neither sow nor reap nor gather into barns, and yet your heavenly Father feeds them. Are you not of more value than they?

Jesus appeals to objective facts about the natural world, including God's providence for animals, and the obvious superiority in value of human beings to those animals, to draw practical conclusion: do not be anxious about your life. This kind of reasoning at least affirms N1. That Jesus even appeals to the realm of nature, rather than simply quoting OT commands or issuing new bald *diktats*, strongly implies support for N2.

Another example of natural law in Jesus' ethics is his famous "Golden Rule" (Matt 7:12): "So whatever you wish that others would do to you, do also to them, for this is the Law and the Prophets." Bockmuehl notes: "The un-complicated assumption of a kind of natural reciprocity and commonality of human needs suggests the acceptance of a moral category that is general and self-evident, rather than positively revealed in the Torah."[1]

This teaching deserves a bit more meditation. Firstly, Jesus teaches his disciples to take their own basic desires as ones that every human being has. Secondly, by telling them to satisfy those basic desires of others, he affirms those desiderata as good. The implication of these two premises is that Jesus teaches all people actually know what is good for them, on some level, since they have desires that ought to be met. Thus in this brief rule, Jesus affirms N1, N2, and N3. And, of course, this rule is known as the "golden rule," partly because it is so foundational (Jesus says it sums up the ethical teaching of the entire OT), but also because examples of it show up in all cultures, albeit in slightly varied forms.

Another famous example of what people now call natural law ethics shows up in Jesus' teaching on sexuality, more specifically divorce. In Mark 10:6–8 and its parallels, Jesus corrects Pharisaical views about this practice by pointing them back to God's originally created order. A

---

[1] Bockmuehl, *Jewish Law*, 118–19.

particular point of grammar in Jesus' appeal makes this clear, appearing in Mark 10:4-9 and Matt 19:4-6 respectively:

> They said, "Moses allowed a man to write a certificate of divorce and to send her away." And Jesus said to them, "Because of your hardness of heart he wrote you this commandment. But from the beginning of creation, 'God made them male and female.' 'Therefore a man shall leave his father and mother and hold fast to his wife, and the two shall become one flesh.' So they are no longer two but one flesh. What therefore God has joined together, let not man separate."

> He answered, "Have you not read that he who created them from the beginning made them male and female, and said, 'Therefore a man shall leave his father and his mother and hold fast to his wife, and the two shall become one flesh'? So they are no longer two but one flesh. What therefore God has joined together, let not man separate."

In both texts, the Greek word απο appears, translated "from." What Jesus' words actually communicate, then, is that God made at the beginning, and continues to make, people male or female. Jesus goes on to explain that this perennial natural reality of two sexes is aimed (Matt 10:7, Mark 19:5; ἕνεκα/ἕνεκεν "therefore") by God at their union. Because this union is God's intention in marriage, Jesus says, we ought not to oppose God's intention by separating these two joined. Thus, the logic of the argument runs like this:

1. God created the male/female order of nature at the beginning in Eden, and he has sustained that order in being since then
2. God's aim in this two-sex order is that the sexes become united in marriage
3. Therefore, since God intends the union of the sexes in marriage, no mere human being ought to break the union when it has been accomplished; that would be to oppose God's intention in nature

At minimum, this affirms N1.

These are by no means the only instances of reasoning from the "objective value" of things in the cosmos in Jesus' teaching, but they are sufficient to demonstrate the point. Jesus' mission was to restore God's world to the Creator's original purposes for it, and his practical guidance constantly directed his disciples to act consistently with this end.

PAUL

Above all figures in Scripture, discussions about natural law in the Bible rightly center on the teaching of the Apostle Paul. This should not surprise us: of all biblical writers, the Apostle to the Gentiles was the one most energetically engaging those who did not have the Torah with the demands of God, and so he was the one most likely to have use of natural law concepts. He mentions the concept "nature" several times, and engages in natural theology and natural law ethics.

Acts 14

After the healing of a crippled man at Lystra, the local inhabitants became convinced Paul and Barnabas were Greek gods. In response to this error, Paul proclaimed (vv. 15-18):

> "Men, why are you doing these things? We also are men, of like nature with you, and we bring you good news, that you should turn from these vain things to a living God, who made the heaven and the earth and the sea and all that is in them. In past generations he allowed all the nations to walk in their own ways. Yet he did not leave himself without witness, for he did good by giving you rains from heaven and fruitful seasons, satisfying your hearts with food and gladness." Even with these words they scarcely restrained the people from offering sacrifice to them.

Paul argues that it is not fitting to worship himself and Barnabas because their nature was merely human.[2] Of course, Paul could have cited the Shema, or the First and Second of the Ten Commandments, but instead he reasoned with the citizens of Lystra based on what was objective in the structure of the world: it was simply a matter of fact that as human beings, Paul and Barnabas were not

---

[2] The Greek word ομοιοπαθεις means "of like passions," but the logic of the argument takes these passions as synecdoche for the whole nature, since the rest of Paul's words do not focus on human passions in contrast to other human features. Rather, the contrast is between created things and the Creator. Perhaps Paul speaks of passions because this feature in particular emphasizes the similarity of human beings with even lower animals, in contrast to the divine nature.

worthy of worship. This assumes N1 clearly and N2, but also perhaps N3, in that Paul expects his hearers to see his argument as sound.

The apostle proclaims the true God to the pagans, and notes that in the past this God let history run largely without interference. He then qualifies this statement, noting that, while 'now' God will not simply let paganism continue, yet even 'before' God was not totally hands off with pagans. Rather, all along God has been testifying to them through nature. According to verse 17, God continually provides "rains from heaven and fruitful seasons, satisfying your hearts with food and gladness." That is, the testimony is the fact that natural processes continue to aim at and reach their appointed goals, and that these goals dovetail together with what human beings need for their own happiness. This testimony makes known a benevolent Creator who deserves our complete devotion. In essence, Paul presents Thomas' "Fifth Way," noted earlier. So, in this text, Paul clearly affirms N1, N2. We can also deduce that this testimony was sufficient to be visible to pagans even in their unregenerate state, for to deny this would be to make Paul's argument to no effect. That is, if this testimony demonstrates that God has revealed himself to the pagans, which is itself a counterpoint to his current demand that they repent, this testimony must not be completely imperceptible to them, just as the call to repentance is not. This implies N3.

Acts 17

The more famous of Paul's "natural theology" speeches in Acts is no doubt his *Aeropagitica*. The most important section of that address for our purposes is (vv. 26–29):

And he made from one man every nation of mankind to live on all the face of the earth, having determined allotted periods and the boundaries of their dwelling place, that they should seek God, and perhaps feel their way toward him and find him. Yet he is actually not far from each one of us, for "in him we live and move and have our being"; as even some of your own poets have said, "For we are indeed his offspring." Being then God's offspring, we ought not to think that the divine being is like gold or silver or stone, an image formed by the art and imagination of man.

Paul quotes Epimenides of Crete and Aratus's *Phainomena* to bolster his Jewish theology, but we need to consider the implications of these citations. Paul regards these writers as expressing truths about the world. This would imply N1, as they are truths about the world, but also N2 and N3, since pagan poets are reporting these truths. Paul then reasons from his natural theology to conclusion against the use of images in worship (verse 29). Again, this must assume N1 at minimum, but since the Apostle was giving an argument to unbelievers, it likely implies N3.

Romans 1:17–32

The *locus classicus* for natural theology, without question, is Romans 1. The apostle makes several facts clear in this stage of his extended argument. In the previous verse, Paul declares the solution to the problem of the whole human race. In verse 17, he begins to state the problem. Later, beginning in chapter 2, he will start to describe the Jewish problem in particular. But in verses 17–32, he focuses on the non-Jewish problem. And that problem is God's wrath, which comes because the Gentiles are sinful. That sinfulness is described in various ways:

- suppressing the truth (18)
- knowing God yet not honouring or giving thanks to him (21)
- exchanging the glory of God for images of creatures (23)

This culpable suppressing of God's revelation leads to further sin, as God withdraws his restraining grace. First it leads to worship of creatures. But it also leads to equally "unnatural" (παρὰ φύσιν) acts–acts which defy the obvious structure of reality just as much as dishonor of the Creator does–on the level of sexual behaviour (24–27). Robert Gagnon's analysis of this text's relation to its preceding context compels agreement. He writes:

> The insertion of 1:25 was Paul's way of reminding the reader of parallels between idolatry and same-sex intercourse that made the punishment so appropriate for the crime. In their vertical relationship to God the gentiles ignored the obvious truth about God visible in creation in order to pursue an absurd course of action–a course of action that they alleged was a product of wise rational reflection. God responded to their idolatry with the punishment of allowing them to debase their bodies in their horizontal relationships with one another. With no divine restraint on their passions, they continued to ignore the obvi-

ous truth–now about heterosexual comple-
mentarity so evident in nature–and pursued
the absurd course of action of having sexual
intercourse with members of the same gender. The correspondences can be laid out as
follows [with "the key parallel being the absurd denial of natural revelation in one's worship of God and intercourse with other humans"]:

idolatry	same-sex intercourse
vertical relationship with God	horizontal relation-ships with each other
suppressing visible evidence in creation	contrary to visible evidence in nature
in the sphere of the mind	in the sphere of body and passions
human decision	divine handing-over
exchange of God for idols	exchange of opposite-sex for same-sex
not glorifying God	dishonoring them-selves
foolish act	self-degrading behav-iour[3]

---

[3] Robert A. J. Gagnon, *The Bible and Homosexual Practice: Texts and Hermeneutics* (Nashville, TN: Abingdon Press, 2003), 267-268.

And it results in the laundry list of sins described in 28-32.

Paul concludes with this statement (32): "Though they know God's righteous decree that those who practice such things deserve to die, they not only do them but give approval to those who practice them." Until this point in his argument (which began in 17), Paul has not used the word "decree." To determine the identity of this decree, then, we need to consider Paul's implied background. The most probable interpretation is that this "decree" is precisely what we call "natural law." Firstly, we should consider that the Greek term Paul uses, δικαίωμα, could be used by someone like Josephus to refer to natural law in *Antiquities* 17.108:

> Although he owned that he was not so much surprised with that thoughtless behavior of his former sons, who were but young, and were besides corrupted by wicked counsellors, who were the occasion of their wiping out of their minds all the righteous dictates of nature, and this out of a desire of coming to the government sooner than they ought to do…[4]

Secondly, we must remember the survey of OT concepts above, and note that the Scriptures described the order present in nature as an expression of God's decree. For example, Psalm 33:6–9[5]:

> By the word of the Lord the heavens were made,

---

[4] William Whiston, trans., *The Works of Josephus: Complete and Unabridged* (Peabody: Hendrickson, 1987).

[5] Cf., e.g., Psalm 148.

and by the breath of his mouth all their host.
He gathers the waters of the sea as a heap;
he puts the deeps in storehouses.
Let all the earth fear the Lord;
let all the inhabitants of the world stand in awe of him!
For he spoke, and it came to be;
he commanded, and it stood firm.

The order of nature, according to Jewish thought, is a manifestation of God's will, God's imperial command. Through its wisdom and logic, one can perceive the will of the Creator. It is this wisdom, this decree, that the Gentiles as a whole have defied.

One part of Romans 1 may seem to suggest an idea contrary to N3: v. 21 which speaks of the thoughts of humanity becoming futile and their hearts becoming darkened. Later in v. 28, Paul speaks similarly of humanity having a "debased mind." We can address this particular counterexample in two ways. First, by returning to the concluding verse, v. 32: whatever gloss we put on this fallen psychology, Paul still concludes his denunciation of the Gentiles by saying that they know these things are wrong. Second, these descriptions of the state of humanity do not actually say that human beings do not know the eternal power and divine nature of God. Certainly, at minimum, they do not say that they are now incapable of ever knowing these things based on reason. Third, within the scope of this passage, one possible understanding of the darkness of the intellect mentioned in this passage comes with the v. 29-31. That is, the "darkness" is manifest in the evil ways people choose to behave. Such behaviour makes no sense in light of God's revealed will (which is what v.

32 is concerned to stress), but people go ahead and choose to do what they know to be senseless anyway. There is a mental and volitional darkness indeed, but it is not, at least in this text, a darkness of complete ignorance about the existence of God or his moral will.

Romans 1, then, affirms N1, N2, and N3. But, before moving on, we should make one further comment. Let us grant, for the sake of argument, that as a small minority of exegetes have argued, this text is not really about natural revelation, but rather special revelation.[6] Still, no interpreter can reasonably deny that Paul is imputing knowledge of God's being and commands to people who are still in unbelief. Thus we cannot say that only regenerate people possess knowledge of God's will. Even if we deny this text supports N1 and N2, it still must support a modified version of N3 in relation to divine positive law. And when we combine this point with the abundant evidence we have already seen for N1, the usual theological motives for denying that this text speaks of natural revelation seem to be undermined.

---

[6] One should note that if the correct translation in 1:20 (contra the majority of scholars) is "things that have been done," the implication is that pagans could not help but infer God's existence from his divine acts in history. It is worth meditating on this fact a little further. How did pagans infer God existed from, say, the events of the Exodus? Well, surely part of the chain of reasoning was the obvious purpose behind the Ten Plagues. These were clearly not "random" natural events. And yet, creation as a whole manifests purpose. If God's existence can be known *a posteriori* through observation of his acts in redemptive history, there should be no reason to say his existence could not be inferred through observation of his normal acts of providence.

Romans 2

If Romans 1 is the *locus classicus* for natural theology, Romans 2 presents the same for natural law especially. However, recent scholars have argued the passage does not refer to this law, and so we will take some space to discuss the matter.

As Douglas Moo points out in his commentary on Romans, v. 12 is part of a defense of God's impartiality following upon the statement of this attribute in vs. 11.[7] Thomas Schreiner in turn notes in his commentary that Paul's point in v. 13 is to show that the Jews are not better off than Gentiles simply because they possess the Torah.[8] He also explains that the main clause of v. 14 is "are a law unto themselves," clarifying the apostle's point: Gentiles possess the law in a certain way as demonstrated by their occasional obedience to it.[9]

In a recent article, C. John Collins provides a strong direct argument that "by nature" must be about the doing of the law, rather than possessing it by nature. He further contends, in fact, that in three phrases Paul is consciously alluding to passages from Aristotle to establish this point. According to his argument, "The three apparent echoes of Aristotle in Romans 2:14–15 are the phrases, they are a law to themselves …, the work of the law…, and accuse or even excuse…," to which he adds, contrary to any suggestion that these are OT phrases: "None of these Greek expressions has an analogue in the LXX."

---

[7] Moo, *The Epistle to the Romans*, 144-145.

[8] Thomas R. Schreiner, *Romans*, Baker Exegetical Commentary on the New Testament (Grand Rapids: Baker Books, 1998), 116–17.

[9] Schreiner, *Romans*, 117.

It is worth summarizing his evidence for these allusions at this juncture. For the first phrase, he cites Aristotle's *Politics* IV.viii.10 (1128a, 31-32): "the refined and free man will have this manner, *being*, as it were, *a law to himself*."[10] He explains Aristotle's argument in context: "The point is that such a person needs no imposed law to make him behave the right way; he has some kind of internal monitor that guides him."[11]

The second phrase, "the work of the law," appears in Aristotle's *The Art of Rhetoric*, I.xv.7 (1375b), which Collins conveys as:

> Further, that justice is real and beneficial, but not that which (only) appears (to be just); nor the written law either, for it does not do *the work of the law*.... And that it belongs to the better man to use and to abide by the unwritten rather than the written (laws). [12]

He once again explains Aristotle's point, and how similar it is to Paul's:

> In context, the expression refers to the *proper* work of the law, that is, the administration of real justice, which often transcends written laws. Aristotle has just argued that we must have recourse to general law and fairness ... as potentially more just than the written law.

---

[10] John C. Collins, "Echoes of Aristotle in Romans 2:14–15: Or, Maybe Abimelech Was Not So Bad After All," *Journal of Markets & Morality* 13, no. 1 (2012): 129.

[11] Collins, "Echoes," 129.

[12] Collins, "Echoes," 130.

> The general law is according to nature ... and
> therefore does not change...

If Paul is using Aristotle's phrase here, he is referring to a kind of justice that transcends the limitations of written laws; this is written on the hearts of the Gentiles to whom Paul has been speaking. This would mean that such people have a perception of what is just that goes beyond whatever written laws they might have.[13]

The last phrase, "accuse or even excuse" finds a parallel according to Collins also in Aristotle's *Rhetoric*, in I.xv.3: "First, then, let us speak of the laws, how one must use (them) when persuading and dissuading, and *accusing and excusing....*"[14]

Collins then addresses the question of whether Paul could plausibly have known Aristotle's works, and whether it is likely his audience could have known them. In defense of both of these claims, he notes evidence that Rome was the main center of study for Aristotle's works by the first century BC: Cicero, Josephus, Justin Martyr, Galen, and Diogenes Laertius all show familiarity with his works. Further, portions of Aristotle's works were accessible in handbook form, and it may be the case that sayings of his had become common in the popular speech of the educated.[15]

Three more points from Collins will solidify his argument. First, he argues, contrary to Schreiner[16]—who nevertheless also concludes that Paul is talking about natu-

---

[13] Collins, "Echoes," 130.

[14] Collins, "Echoes," 130.

[15] Collins, "Echoes," 131.

[16] Schreiner, *Romans*, 122.

ral law here[17]—that Paul is alluding to Jeremiah 31's promise of a new covenant. Yet, Collins argues that Paul is alluding to it not to indicate that these Gentiles are the real fulfillment of it. On the contrary, Paul's point is that their occasional obedience to natural law (as evidenced in Aristotle's reflection on this reality), set in contrast to the Jews' obvious continuing sinfulness, is an ironic proof against the possibility that the new covenant had already been fulfilled in the Jewish people prior to Jesus. The Jewish people were not morally outstanding in Paul's day, as they would be if the new covenant had truly been established. The reality was that sometimes the Gentiles were more virtuous in their obedience to natural law than the Jews were.[18]

Second, Collins provides some extended evidence for goodness among Gentiles that both supports his argument and also our larger one. He is worth quoting at length in this regard:

> The Old Testament has several ways of portraying Gentiles who show a sound moral sense. To begin with, there is the allowance of moral perception—even to the point of adopting sound insights into the authorized religion of Israel (Ex. 18, the advice of Jethro; Prov. 31:1–9). If it was the case that New Testament *Haustafeln* derived something of their form and content from Hellenistic analogues, this would reflect a similar outlook. Certainly the stress on a good reputation

---

[17] Schreiner, *Romans*, 124.

[18] Collins, "Echoes," 143.

among unbelievers (e.g., 1 Tim. 3:7; 1 Peter 2:12–15) assumes some level of moral perception among their neighbors, as does the task of the governing authorities (Rom. 13:1–7).

Second, there are clear instances in which the biblical authors describe the moral performance of the Gentiles as a way of contrasting that with the moral underachievement of some Israelites; for example, Genesis 12:18–19, Pharaoh upbraids Abram on moral grounds; 20:1–18, Abimelech pleads innocence and upbraids Abraham; cf. 21:22–34; 26:6–11, 23–33; 38:26, Judah acknowledges that Tamar is more righteous than he; 1 Samuel 6:1–9, the Philistine clergy show deeper insight into God's presence than the Israelites had done; Jeremiah 39:11–14, Nebuchadnezzar showed more concern for Jeremiah's well-being than Zedekiah had done; Ezekiel 5:6–8, the people of Jerusalem have not even acted according to the rules of the nations around them; Jonah 1:11–14, the Phoenician sailors do not want to be guilty of Jonah's blood. The implication is that one had a right to expect more of the Israelite. This is probably Paul's implication in 1 Corinthians 5:1 (sexual immorality of a kind that is not tolerated even among pagans).[19]

Third, and last, Collins provides a grammatical argument that "by nature" should go with the 'doing' rather

---

[19] Collins, "Echoes," 141–42.

than the 'having' of v. 14. He notes that syntax of the sentence should incline us to this position, as *phusei* occurs outside the attributive phrase, that if Paul had wanted to link the word with 'having' he could have written it differently (he gives Gal. 4:8 as an example), and that Chrysostom, whose native tongue was Greek, supports this gloss.[20]

Though a few have intended to argue for it,[21] John Murray provides a strong argument that the "nature" in question is not that of regenerate Christians:

> Paul does not say that the law is written upon their hearts. He refrains from this form of statement apparently for the same reason as in verse 14 he had said that the Gentiles "do the things of the law" and not that they did or fulfilled the law. Such expressions as "fulfilling the law" and "the law written upon the heart" are reserved for a state of heart and mind will far beyond that predicated of unbelieving Gentiles.[22]

There is therefore good reason to defend the traditional interpretation of Rom. 2:14 as referring to the occasional obedience of unbelieving Gentiles to natural law inscribed upon their hearts. However, if contemporary New Testament scholars such as N. T. Wright[23] and Dr.

---

[20] Collins, "Echoes," 144.

[21] Dr. Collins mentions some including Dr. Simon Gathercole ("Echoes," 162n78).

[22] John Murray, *The Epistle to the Romans*, 74-75.

[23] See Dr. Wright's Romans commentary: "The Letter to the Romans," in *The New Interpreter's Bible, Vol. 10: Acts, Romans, 1 Corinthians*, ed. Leander E. Keck (Nashville, TN: Abingdon Press, 2002), 393–770.

Simon Gathercole are correct, and this instead refers to a genuine fulfillment of Jeremiah's new covenant prophecy, this would of course not undermine the rest of the present book's argument. If, as Wright argues, Rom 2:14 speaks of the "Gentiles who do not have the law by nature," in contrast, implicitly, to the Jews who do have the Torah by "nature,"[24] then Paul's language fits neatly into the scholastic category of "second nature," which is a kind of habit or custom. Race or ethnicity, with its complex history and social practices, is something one is born into (like true nature), and something that powerfully shapes the kind of persons that people become. [25] Thus individuals of the Jewish nation, by virtue of their social history, in this sense possess their heritage, especially the Torah, by (second) nature.

Yet this does not imply that everything Paul, or the Bible, describes as "nature" is socially constructed the way that culture is. Quite clearly in Paul's mind, the nature of the sexes is an example of something God created in Genesis 1 and 2. Robert Gagnon's *The Bible and Homosexual Practice* shows how Paul is alluding to the creation narrative while he speaks of homosexuality,[26] revealing how closely

---

[24] Galatians 2:15 probably uses φυσις in the same way as the present text.

[25] In this case, conforming to the first definition of φυσις offered by BDAG: "condition or circumstance as determined by birth, natural endowment/condition."

[26] Gagnon provides a decisive argument demonstrating Paul intentionally alludes to the creation narrative of Genesis in his description of homosexuality in 1:24–27. Some of the probative evidence: (1) Paul traces sin back to the fall, bringing Genesis 1 to mind; (2) he writes "ever since the creation of the world" (1:20); (3) he refers to the "Creator" (1:25) (4) he denotes the sexes with the terms θήλειαι and ἄρσενες rather than γυναῖκες and ἄνδρες or ἄνθρωποι, following

God's original creational intentions and the nature of the sexes are bound together in the apostle's mind. And further, to suggest that, for Paul, the creation order we have been discussing throughout this essay is entirely socially constructed would be just for him to deny there is any creation order at all. Clearly, the apostle means something other than that.

Romans 13

As mentioned in a quote from Collins above, and as noted in a previous Davenant Guide, *Jesus and Pacifism*, Romans 13 entails that unbelieving Gentiles can know and enact justice to an imperfect but real degree. We need not recount the full treatment given to the text in that book, but we can make a few notes on the significance of Paul's teaching on the magistrate for our present question. To clarify the argument, let us set the text before us (vs. 1-4):

---

the LXX of Gen 1:27 exactly; (5) the apostle provides a threefold reference of birds/animals/reptiles which appears in Gen 1:30; (6) possibly "the lie" (Rom 1:25) alludes to humanity's original false implication about God in the fall, agreeing with the Serpent's lies; (7) "shame" appears in Genesis (Rom 1:27, cf. Gen 3:1, 8), (8) as does knowledge (Rom 1:19, 28, 32; cf. the Tree of Knowledge), (9) and the sentence of death (Rom 1:32; cf. Gen 2:17; 3:4-5, 20, 23) (290-291). Gagnon writes: "For Paul, both idolatry and same-sex intercourse reject God's verdict that what was made and arranged was 'very good'" (1:31). Humanity rejected the goodness of God for idolatry, rejected dominion for the worship of animals, and rejected their dimorphic sexuality for homosexual acts contrary to nature (291). "As with Jesus, so with Paul: the creation story in Genesis does not leave room for a legitimate expression of same-sex intercourse. Even though Rom 1:18–32 speaks of events after the fall, for Paul all human rebellions are in one way or another rebellions against God's will for humankind set in motion at creation" (291).

Let every person be subject to the governing authorities. For there is no authority except from God, and those that exist have been instituted by God. Therefore whoever resists the authorities resists what God has appointed, and those who resist will incur judgment. For rulers are not a terror to good conduct, but to bad. Would you have no fear of the one who is in authority? Then do what is good, and you will receive his approval, for he is God's servant for your good. But if you do wrong, be afraid, for he does not bear the sword in vain. For he is the servant of God, an avenger who carries out God's wrath on the wrongdoer.

It is not difficult to see how this text affirms N1: Paul tells us outright that God has put political order into the world, and that disobeying it is wrong. But further, we must remember that the authorities the apostle is speaking about here are themselves not Christians at all. Yet, he teaches, they approve what is good and avenge wrongdoing. Though the text does not say this explicitly, it seems fair to assume Paul agreed that magistrates did this deliberately, not by some happy coincidence. That is, this text implies the non-Christians magistrates know good and evil, and respond accordingly in law. This entails N2 and N3.

Now, it does not take much familiarity with human history to realize that governments do not constantly and unfailingly behave in the way the apostle speaks here. This is not strictly speaking a problem for the present argument, but is rather a question about the veracity of the text itself. Nevertheless, it may help to address this question briefly, and indeed, the most likely reply only strengthens the case for natural law. The best resolution is to recognize that Paul is speaking here of the ideal form of the government, a description of what God's design is for the state in its nature and function. Yet, as with human behaviour in general, so in the political behaviour of the magistrates in particular, people fall short of the glory of God. We can fail to obey natural law, and this is what happens when magistrates decree unjustly. Nevertheless, it is still true that, fundamentally, states are meant to perform the task Paul describes here, and so the apostle is right to speak of the ideal as he does.

Ephesians 2

In the midst of a description of the state of fallen humanity, Paul speaks of how we (vs. 3) "were by nature children of wrath, like the rest of mankind." At first glance, this text may seem to indicate this book's perspective on nature in the Bible is mistaken, for thus far we have treated it as a reflection of God's design, and moral will. Yet this text obviously is not using it in this way, but rather as a reference to the condition his readers (and by extension, humanity) were born into as children of human beings. But in fact such a use of the concept of nature is consistent with the classical perspective on natural law we have been arguing is biblical. More specifically, this is a case of what the scholastics would call "second nature," which would often be tied to race and culture. However, unlike race, Paul now speaks of a different kind of construction: sin. In fact, it would be more accurate to call this a destruction, for that is what sin really is. Sin is a habit all human beings possess from birth that drags human beings away from their God-intended telos, and towards utter ruin. This propensity towards evil consequently calls down the wrath of God, and hence by (second) nature we are subject to God's wrath.

1 Corinthians 6

Returning to positive proof for natural law in Pauline ethics, 1 Cor 6:18 provides a good example of the concept without the word. The apostle writes that "the sexually immoral person sins against his own body." In other words, to sin sexually is to offend against the right order inscribed by God into the body he created for human beings. It breaks the natural law God decreed. This proves N1, though not N2 or N3.

1 Corinthians 11

The other frequently discussed Pauline text on natural law comes in the apostle's teachings on head-coverings. Paul writes (1 Cor. 11:13–15):

> Judge for yourselves: is it proper for a wife to pray to God with her head uncovered? Does not nature itself teach you that if a man wears long hair it is a disgrace for him, but if a woman has long hair, it is her glory? For her hair is given to her for a covering.

Bockmuehl provides what is probably the correct explanation of this text:

> The particular argument of this passage, however, derives from the fact that in this context the perversion of hairstyles denoted a perver-

sion of sexual identity. For a man to wear female hairstyle was a way of communicating effeminacy and thus homosexuality. It is likely, therefore, that for Paul men's long hair is 'unnatural' not just by common convention or sentiment, but especially because of what it is perceived to denote in the moral realm. As we saw in Romans 1, both Paul and Hellenistic Judaism decried homosexual acts as intrinsically contrary to the created order.[27]

To attempt to elaborate: the created order implies homosexual actions of any kind are unnatural. That is, not simply homosexual acts, but behaviour in general that today might be called "gender bending." Rather, according to Jews and Christians, nature teaches that people should behave as the sex they are. But of course, no one lives as a sexed being in isolation; all people must participate in societies, which have socially established conventions for the sexes. Thus, nature dictates that people behave as their own sex in relation to others in society, and thus behave according to the social conventions for sexes established by the society they are in.[28] The present text addresses one such convention, that of hairstyle.[29]

---

[27] Bockmuehl, *Jewish Law*, 134.

[28] The obvious OT background text for Paul's logic would be Deuteronomy 22:5: "A woman shall not wear a man's garment [literally, "things", not just clothes], nor shall a man put on a woman's cloak, for whoever does these things is an abomination to the Lord your God." Deuteronomy is also concerned that men and women dress in clothing styles as society has established their own sex ought to.

[29] For an example of a pagan supporter of natural law making a similar argument, see Seneca, *Epistle* 122.7.

Of course, social conventions can require sin, and Paul cannot be ignorant of this fact. But he also, apparently, does not consider women wearing conventional female hairstyles (nor men male ones) and veils to be a sinful custom on the part of culture.

JUDE

The last text in our survey shall be Jude 7. The brother of James writes that the inhabitants of Sodom and its surrounding cities "pursued other flesh." The ESV not unreasonably paraphrases this "pursued unnatural desire," as the sexual sins Genesis narrates included desires for homosexual intercourse and for rape. Jude writes that those cities stand as an example of punishment for that behaviour. This implies N1, and assuming God does not punish people for disobeying orders of which they were invincibly ignorant, it would seem to imply N2 and N3 as well.

X:
CONCLUDING THOUGHTS

HAVING now completed our survey of the Old Testament, extracanonical Jewish Literature, and New Testament texts, we propose that we have successfully demonstrated that <u>natural law is woven deeply into the fabric of biblical teaching</u>, especially the notion of an objective order for the universe, including a moral order, framed by God and discernible by all men. But what is the value of this survey, if correct?

APOLOGETIC BENEFIT

Recognizing that the divine positive laws revealed in Scripture correlate and complement the objective order God has installed in creation helps to show God is good. If Scripture recognizes and supports natural law, then the God of Scripture must intend to bless and perfect us according to the nature we know in our bones, otherwise the expression "God is good" is but a tautology. And indeed, when we look at the commands God gives us in Scripture, we see they consist with the best moral instincts of the human race; likewise, when we see the promises of blessing God gives, we perceive the completion of our natures.

Seeing Scripture as supporting a natural law theory also helps Christian ethicists concerned with obedience to special revelation see the direction in which their thinking needs to go. That is, Christians who believe in Scripture ought to be defending the existence and visibility of natural law, both to other Christians and to the world at large.

BEST EXPLANATION OF EARLY CHURCH HISTORY

Additionally, this perspective on natural law helps make sense of historical data. More specifically, it makes it easy to understand how from its inception, Christianity assumed and supported the doctrine of natural law. It is also what we would expect, given the social context of the early Christians. As mentioned earlier, Bockmuehl discusses why Christians would be interested in using natural law reasoning:

> At the same time, and in spite of justified modern philosophical and theological qualms,[1] Graeco-Roman and NT authors in their different ways confirm the antiquity of both the substance and the terminology of Natural Law discourse. Most ancient writers shared the unquestioned assumption that humanity's place in the social and natural order implied fundamental principles of morality; and that these were continuous with all good systems of positive law, and recognized by cultured peoples everywhere. Not only the

---

[1] On this point, of course, I would part ways with Dr. Bockmuehl.

Greeks and Romans but Jews and Christians, too, argued in such terms, if only to make their moral discourse possible in an intercultural world. Their theologically based presupposition of a universal ontology, moreover, served as the indispensable framework for their covenantal worldview.[2]

IMPLICATIONS FOR MISSIONS AND PHILOSOPHY

The penultimate sentence here raises another reason why this conclusion is beneficial: it means the Bible allows cultural engagement, and more specifically of a kind that can admit goodness and value outside the visible church. For Christians especially interested in being "missional," this cannot but be useful. This conclusion also permits Bible believers to recognize the fact of the *philosophia perennis*. In addition to the appendix of *The Abolition of Man* (mentioned above), which shows a great deal of agreement on practical wisdom across time and geography, C.S. Lewis also recounts how several major religious and philosophical traditions all recognized the existence of natural law in the abstract:

> St Augustine defines virtue as *ordo amoris*, the ordinate condition of the affections in which every object is accorded that kind of degree of love which is appropriate to it. Aristotle says that the aim of education is to make the pupil

---

[2] Bockmuehl, *Jewish Law*, 116.

like and dislike what he ought. When the age for reflective thought comes, the pupil who has been thus trained in 'ordinate affections' or 'just sentiments' will easily find the first principles in Ethics; but to the corrupt man they will never be visible at all and he can make no progress in that science. Plato before him had said the same. The little human animal will not at first have the right responses. It must be trained to feel pleasure, liking, disgust, and hatred at those things which really are pleasant, likeable, disgusting and hateful. In the *Republic*, the well-nurtured youth is one 'who would see most clearly whatever was amiss in ill-made works of man or ill-grown works of nature, and with a just distaste would blame and hate the ugly even from his earliest years and would give delighted praise to beauty, receiving it into his soul and being nourished by it, so that he becomes a man of gentle heart. All this before he is of an age to reason; so that when Reason at length comes to him, then, bred as he has been, he will hold out his hands in welcome and recognize her because of the affinity he bears to her.' In early Hinduism that conduct in men which can be called good consists in conformity to, or almost participation in, the *Rta*—that great ritual or pattern of nature and supernature which is revealed alike in the cosmic order, the moral virtues, and the ceremonial of the temple. Righteousness, correctness, order, the

Rta, is constantly identified with *satya* or truth, correspondence to reality. As Plato said that the Good was 'beyond existence' and Wordsworth that through virtue the stars were strong, so the Indian masters say that the gods themselves are born of the *Rta* and obey it.

The Chinese also speak of a great thing (the greatest thing) called the *Tao*. It is the reality beyond all predicates, the abyss that was before the Creator Himself. It is Nature, it is the Way, the Road. It is the Way in which the universe goes on, the Way in which things everlastingly emerge, stilly and tranquilly, into space and time. It is also the Way which every man should tread in imitation of that cosmic and supercosmic progression, conforming all activities to that great exemplar. 'In ritual', say the *Analects*, 'it is harmony with Nature that is prized.' The ancient Jews likewise praise the law as being 'true.'[3]

BIBLICAL FOUNDATION FOR PROTESTANT CHRISTENDOM

To see the Bible as supporting natural law means that the unique civilization that two-kingdoms Protestantism contributed to is not undermined by Scripture. The precisianists and Anabaptists were wrong to deny that any just po-

---

[3] C. S. Lewis, *The Abolition of Man* (1944; repr., New York: HarperOne, 2000), 16-18.

litical order could be founded that did not submit to their private and special revelation, since justice can be known from the wisdom in God's good creation. Natural law also frees up the civil magistrate to carry out his office apart from subordination to the clergy, since he is equipped to reason justly, thus making sense out of those biblical passages like Romans 13:1-7.

CLARIFYING EXEGETICAL ISSUES

Realizing that the Bible assumes knowledge of the natural law may also help us in exegetical quandaries that continue to puzzle Bible scholars to this day. More specifically: how do we explain the logic of Jesus and Paul, when they declare some parts of the Torah no longer binding on Christians (e.g., Sabbath and Kosher laws), but other parts still in force (e.g., laws against sexual immorality)? Natural law may provide the key here, in that the former examples are clearly "socially constructed" (even if divinely so), and the writers of Scripture explicitly note this. Paul expresses what is surely his own view of holy days in Rom 14:5 when he says "all days [are] alike." There is nothing in the nature of Saturday (or Sunday) which differs from any other day of the week. And, as Bockmuehl notes, Jesus makes a sort of natural law argument when discussing Kosher food laws:

> Jesus' clinching statement is what might be called an argument from 'the way things are', namely that unclean foods enter not the heart but the stomach before being expelled again, into the sewer (Mark 7.19). The created order itself shows that contaminated foods merely

pass through the body and do not affect the
heart, but evil has its very seat in the heart and
comes from within.[4]

Of course, Jesus knew God had instituted Kosher
laws as an enacted symbolic lesson, but that is the point.
The Torah was intended to symbolize a future something,
and Jesus was bringing that something into reality in his
own ministry, making the symbols no longer necessary.
Once that symbolic reason for the law no longer applied,
the laws were no longer necessary. That is, unless natural
law required them. And so Jesus' pointing out that, in fact,
natural law does not require obedience to Kosher law
means that the laws are no longer binding as a result of his
ministry. On the other hand, as we have noted, the apostle
Paul and others do seem to apply some Old Testament
laws to Christians, for example in the realm of sexual ethics. But sexual immorality clearly does defy the natural
purpose of the sexes, and harms human beings as such.[5]

In light of these things, is it possible that, aside from
a handful of commands that require ritual acts of Chris-

---

[4] Bockmuehl, *Jewish Law*, 119. Note that God makes the same argument
to Peter in Acts 10:15. According to the order of nature, all things are
good. The Torah set out symbolic laws which are no longer in force,
and those laws were never strictly republications of natural law.

[5] My analysis of Jesus' reasoning on divorce earlier corroborates this
hypothesis: he seems to base his teaching on the subject on the created
order/natural law. Several texts in Scripture focused on sexual ethics
outside the realm of sexual intercourse also seem to follow a similar
pattern (e.g., Paul's reasoning about gender roles appeals to the original
creation order). And, as I also noted earlier, the texts which speak of
homosexuality refer to natural law, and so support this hermeneutical
suggestion.

tians (e.g., Baptism and the Eucharist),[6] the rest of New Testament "law" is simply expressing what natural law and prudence already demand?[7] If so, we may be able to get a new handle on the logic of NT ethics as a whole, without trying to treat it as casuistry based on a positive law code somehow vaguely different from an OT positive law code. Of course, this way of thinking isn't really new at all, for Protestant legal scholars such as Girolamo Zanchi already reached the same conclusion centuries ago:

> Thus the Jews at the time of the apostles sinned in two respects when they wanted to subject Gentiles who converted to Christ to the Mosaic law: because the Gentiles had never been obligated by this law, and it did not apply to them at all because Christ himself had freed even the Jews from this law. How great is the iniquity, then, if Christians want to subject people today, Gentiles and magistrates, to Judaic law? As long as those laws were handed down to the Israelites, they

---

[6] Even these laws, in a secondary sense, are an expression of natural law. For an interesting reflection along these lines regarding the Eucharist, see Dr. Peter Leithart's, *Against Christianity* (Moscow, ID: Canon Press, 2003), 84, who cites Aquinas citing Augustine, explaining that "no religious body or group can exist without signs and symbols." Thus, if God wants a visible community, natural law requires that he institute some symbols.

[7] Of course, many obligations fall under the heading of "prudence." This includes the obligation to act in accord with facts once they are recognized. And this will include facts of history, and most importantly, facts about what the Creator has done in history. And, still further, among these historical acts are God's communicative acts otherwise known as the inspired Scriptures. Once these are known, the demands of prudence require belief in the Bible in its entirety. Yet, none of this undoes my main point.

did not apply to the Gentiles. It is only when they coincide with Natural Law and were confirmed by Christ himself that they apply to all people.[8]

THE CHRISTIAN LIFE AS MATURE REFLECTION

And this leads to one final reflection on the value of these conclusions. The Bible constantly describes the New Covenant era as a time in which people will have knowledge of God and his will in a direct and mature way. All people will know God, and teachers will not be needed. Now, while clearly these blessings of the New Covenant have not come in their fullness, still, it is just as clear that our Lord intended us to experience them more than Old Covenant Israel did. He taught his disciples that, at the point of his death and beyond, he no longer considered them mere servants, but his friends, because they finally grasped his intentions. And this cannot only describe the Twelve, for Paul also draws the contrast between Old and New Covenant as between a child under a tutor and a grown, mature son. If the reflection on exegetical issues immediately above is correct, this nature of the New Covenant makes sense. For, apart from a few commands, the "law" of the New Covenant is nothing other than the law of love, which is just to will good for others, where "good" is defined by the structure of their being. In other words, almost the entirety of God's demand for New Covenant believers is simply to obey the law of their own being, their

---

[8] Girolamo Zanchi, *On the Law in General*, translated and edited by Jeffrey J. Veenstra, Sources in Early Modern Economics, Ethics, and Law (Grand Rapids: Christian's Library Press, 2012), 81.

own flourishing. And this is really like being under no law at all, at least not any more than St. Augustine's memorable advice to those seeking God's guidance for their lives:

> See what we are insisting upon; that the deeds of men are only discerned by the root of charity. For many things may be done that have a good appearance, and yet proceed not from the root of charity. For thorns also have flowers: some actions truly seem rough, seem savage; howbeit they are done for discipline at the bidding of charity. Once for all, then, a short precept is given thee: Love, and do what thou wilt: whether thou hold thy peace, through love hold thy peace; whether thou cry out, through love cry out; whether thou correct, through love correct; whether thou spare, through love do thou spare: let the root of love be within, of this root can nothing spring but what is good.[9]

---

[9] Augustine, "Homily 7 on the First Epistle of John," in *Homilies on First John*, New Advent, http://www.newadvent.org/fathers/170207.htm.

BIBLIOGRAPHY

Augustine. "Homily 7 on the First Epistle of John." In
    Homilies on First John, New Advent,
    http://www.newadvent.org/fathers/170207.htm.

Aquinas, Thomas. *Commentary on Aristotle's* Nicomachean
    Ethics. Revised edition, translated by C. J. Litzinger.
    Notre Dame, IN: Dumb Ox Books, 1993.

_____. *On Being and Essence*. Translated by Armand Maurer.
    2nd ed. Toronto, ON: PIMS, 1968.

Summa Theologiae. Translated by Fathers of the English
    Dominican Province. Notre Dame, IN: Ave Maria
    Press, 1948.

Aristotle. *Nicomachean Ethics*. Translated by W. D. Ross, ed.
    J. O. Urmson. In vol. 2 of *The Complete Works of
    Aristotle*, edited by Jonathan Barnes, 1729-1867. 2nd
    ed. 1984; repr., Princeton, NJ: Princeton University
    Press, 1995.

Augustine. *The Confessions*. Edited by Robert Maynard
    Hutchins, and translated by Edward Bouverie Pusey.
    In *Augustine*, vol. 18 of *Great Books of the Western
    World*. 1952; repr., Chicago: Encyclopedia Britannica,
    1988.

Barr, James. *Biblical Faith and Natural Theology: The Gifford Lectures for 1991: Delivered in the University of Edinburgh.* Oxford: OUP, 1993.

Barth, Karl. *Church Dogmatics.* Translated by Bromiley, Campbell, Wilson, McNab, Knight, and Stewart, and edited by G.W. Bromiley and T.F. Torrance. Peabody, MA: Hendrickson Publishers, 2010.

Baur, Michael. "Law and Natural Law." In *The Oxford Handbook of Aquinas,* edited by Brian Davies & Eleonore Stump, 238-254. Oxford: OUP, 2014.

Bockmuehl, Markus. *Jewish Law in Gentile Churches: Halakhah and the Beginning of Christian Public Ethics.* Grand Rapids: T & T Clark, 2003.

Bohner, Philotheus. "The Realistic Conceptualism of William Ockham." *Traditio* 4 (1946): 307-335.

Bright, John. *Jeremiah: Introduction, Translation, and Notes.* Garden City, NY: Doubleday, 1965.

Bruce, F. F. *The Epistle of Paul to the Romans: An Introduction and Commentary.* Revised edition. 1985; repr., Grand Rapids: Wm. B. Eerdmans Publishing, 2003.

Budziszewski, J. *The Line Through the Heart: Natural Law as Fact, Theory, and Sign of Contradiction.* Wilmington, DE: ISI Books, 2011.

Burns, J. Patout, Jr., trans., and ed. *Romans: Interpreted by Early Christian Commentators.* Grand Rapids: Wm. B. Eerdman's Publishing, 2012.

Calvin, Jehan. *Commentaires sur l'épistre aux Romains,* in tome 3 of *Commentaires de Jehan Calvin sur le Nouveau Testament.* Paris: Librairie de Ch. Meyrueis et co., 1855.

Chadwick, G. A. *The Book of Exodus.* London: Hodder and Stoughton, 1898.

Charlesworth, James H. *The Old Testament Pseudepigrapha, Volume 1: Apocalyptic Literature and Testaments.* New York; London: Yale University Press, 1983.

_____. *The Old Testament Pseudepigrapha and the New Testament, Volume 2: Expansions of the "Old Testament" and Legends, Wisdom, and Philosophical Literature, Prayers, Psalms and Odes, Fragments of Lost Judeo-Hellenistic Works.* New Haven, CT: Yale University Press, 1985.

Chrysostome, Jean. *Homilies sur l'épître aux Romains.* Translated by Abbé J. Bareille. Vol. 8 of des *Œuvres Complètes de S. Jean Chrysostome.* Paris: Librairie de Louis Vives, 1871.

Collins, John C. "Echoes of Aristotle in Romans 2:14–15: Or, Maybe Abimelech Was Not So Bad After All." *Journal of Markets & Morality* 13, no. 1 (Spring 2010): 123-173.

Collins, John J. *Encounters with Biblical Theology.* Minneapolis: Fortress Press, 2005.

De Libera, Alain. "Question de réalisme. Sur deux arguments anti-ockhamistes de John Sharpe." *Revue de Métaphysique et de Morale* 97e Année, no. 1, Les Universaux (Janvier-mars1992): 83-110.

Feser, Edward. *Aquinas: Beginner's Guides.* 2009; repr., Oxford: Oneworld Publications, 2010.

_____. *Scholastic Metaphysics: A Contemporary Introduction.* Germany: Editionses Scholasticae, 2014.

Forde, Steven. "Hugo Grotius on Ethics and War." *American Political Science Review* 92, no. 3 (Sept. 1998): 639-48.

Gagnon, Robert A. J. *The Bible and Homosexual Practice: Texts and Hermeneutics.* Nashville, TN: Abingdon Press, 2003.

Gilson, Étienne. *Being and Some Philosophers*. 2nd ed. Toronto, ON: Pontifical Institute of Mediaeval Studies, 1952.

_____. *Le Réalisme Méthodique*. 2e ed. Paris : Chez Pierre Téqui, 1937.

_____. *Moral Values and the Moral Life: The Ethical Theory of St. Thomas Aquinas*. Translated by Leo Richard Ward. Hamden, CT: The Shoe String Press, 1961.

Gregory Nazianzus. *On Theology*. In *Five Theologial Orations*, translated by Stephen Reynolds. Estate of Stephen Reynolds, 2011.

Gregory of Nyssa. *The Great Catechism*. In Series 2 of the *Nicene and Post-Nicene Fathers*, edited by Philip Schaff. NY: Christian Literature Publishing, 1892.

Grenz, Stanley. *The Moral Quest: Foundations for Christian Ethics*. Downers Grove, IL: InterVarsity Press, 1997.

Grotius, Hugo. *On the Rights of War and Peace: An Abridged Translation*. Translated and edited by William Whewell. Cambridge: John W. Parker, 1853.

Gudorf, Christine. "The Erosion of Sexual Dimorphism." *Journal of the American Academy of Religion* 69, no. 4 (Dec. 2001): 863-892.

Haldane, Robert. *An Exposition of the Epistle to the Romans*. Florida: Mac Donald Publishing Company, 1958.

Harrison, R. K., ed. *The Encyclopedia of Biblical Ethics*. New York: Testament Books, 1992.

Hauerwas, Stanley. *The Peaceable Kingdom: A Primer in Christian Ethics*. Notre Dame, IN: University of Notre Dame Press, 1983.

Henry, Carl F. H. "Natural Law and a Nihilistic Culture."
  First Things 49 (January 1995): 58.
  www.firstthings.com/article/1995/01/natural-law-
  and-a-nihilistic-culture.

Hodge, Charles. *A Commentary on Romans.* Revised edition.
  1864; repr., Carlisle, PA: Banner of Truth Trust,
  1975.

Holmes, Arthur F. *Ethics: Approaching Moral Decisions.*
  Downers Grove, IL: InterVarsity Press, 1984.

Hooker, Richard. *Divine Law and Human Nature: Or, the first
  book of Of the Laws of Ecclesiastical Polity, Concerning Laws
  and their Several Kinds in General.* Edited/translated by
  W. Bradford Littlejohn, Brian Marr, and Bradley
  Belschner. Moscow, ID: The Davenant Press, 2017.

Jordan, James B. *Studies in Food and Faith.* Tyler, TX: Biblical Horizions, 1989. Digital Version.

Keyser, Herman J. *A Commentary on Exodus.* Grand Rapids:
  Zondervan, 1940.

Kidner, Derek. *Psalms 1-72: An Introduction and Commentary.*
  Downers' Grove, IL: InterVarsity Press, 1973.

Kreeft, Peter. *Making Sense out of Suffering.* Ann Arbor, MI:
  Servant Books, 1986.

Leithart, Peter. *Against Christianity.* Moscow, ID: Canon
  Press, 2003.

Lewis, C. S. *The Abolition of Man.* New York: HarperOne,
  2000.

Luscombe, David E. "Natural Morality and Natural Law."
  In *The Cambridge History of Later Medieval Philosophy*, ed-
  ited by Norman Kretzmann, Anthony Kenny, and
  Jan Pinborg, 705-721. 1982; Cambridge: CUP, 2000.

Luther, Martin. *Commentary on the Epistle to the Romans.* Translated by J. Theodore Mueller. 1954; repr., Grand Rapids: Kregel Publications, 1979.

Mangina, Joseph L. *Karl Barth: Theologian of Christian Witness.* Louisville, KY: Westminster John Knox Press, 2004.

Maritain, Jacques. *Natural Law: Reflections on Theory and Practice.* Edited by William Sweet. South Bend, IN: St. Augustine's Press, 2001.

_____. *Philosophy of Nature.* Translated by Imelda C. Byrne. New York: The Philosophical Library, 1951.

Marshall, Wallace W. *Puritanism and Natural Theology.* Eugene, OR: Pickwick Publications, 2016.

McCord-Adams, Marilyn. "Ockham's Nominalism and Unreal Entities." *The Philosophical Review* 86, no. 2 (April 1977): 144-176.

McInerny, Ralph. "Ethics." In *The Cambridge Companion to Aquinas,* edited by Norman Kretzmann and Eleonore Stump, 196-216. Cambridge: CUP, 2005.

Moo, Douglas. *The Epistle to the Romans.* New International Commentary on the New Testament. Grand Rapids: Wm. B. Eerdmans Publishing, 1996.

Motyer, J. Alec. *The Prophecy of Isaiah: An Introduction & Commentary.* Downers' Grove, IL: InterVarsity Press, 1993.

Murray, John. *The Epistle to the Romans.* Grand Rapids: Wm. B. Eerdmans Publishing, 1968.

Oderberg, David S. *Real Essentialism.* New York: Routledge, 2007.

Oswalt, John N. *The Book of Isaiah: Chapters 40-66*, New International Commentary on the New Testament. Grand Rapids: Wm. B. Eerdmans Publishing, 1998.

Pinckaers, Servais. *The Sources of Christian Ethics*. Translated by Mary Thomas Noble 3rd ed. Washington, DC: CUA Press, 1995.

Plato, *Parmenides*. Translated by Mary Louise Gill and Paul Ryan. Indianapolis, IN: Hackett, 1996.

Rattigan, William. "Hugo Grotius." *Journal of the Society of Comparative Legislation* 6, no. 1 (1905): 68-81.

Schaff, Philip. *The History of Creeds*. Vol. 1 of *The Creeds of Christendom*, edited by David S. Schaff. 6th ed. 1983; repr., Grand Rapids: Baker Books, 2007.

_____. *The Evangelical Protestant Creeds*. Vol. 3 of *The Creeds of Christendom*, edited by David S. Schaff. 6th ed. 1983; repr., Grand Rapids: Baker Books, 2007.

Schreiner, Thomas R. *Romans*. Baker Exegetical Commentary on the New Testament. Grand Rapids: Baker Books, 1998.

Sertillanges, A.G. *La Philosophie Morale de St. Thomas d'Aquin*. 2e ed. Paris: Éditions Montaigne, 1946.

Skehan, Patrick W., and Alexander A. Di Lella, O.F.M. *The Wisdom of Ben Sira: A New Translation With Notes, Introduction and Commentary*. Vol. 39 of the Anchor Yale Bible. New Haven, CT: Yale University Press, 2008.

Smick, Elmer B. "Job." In *The Expositor's Bible Commentary: 1 & 2 Kings, 2 & 2 Chronicles, Ezra, Nehemiah, Esther, Job*, edited by Frank E. Gaebelein, 843-1060. Grand Rapids: Zondervan Publishing House, 1988.

Turretin, Francis. *Institutes of Elenctic Theology*. Translated by George Musgrave Giger, and edited by James T. Dennison, Jr. Phillipsburg, NJ: P&R Publishing, 1992.

Van Til, Cornelius. *Christian Apologetics*. Edited by William Edgar. 2nd ed. Phillipsburg, NJ: P&R Publishing, 2003.

_____. *The Defense of the Faith*. Edited by K. Scott Oliphint. 4th ed. Phillipsburg, NJ: P&R Publishing, 2008.

Veatch, Henry. *Realism and Nominalism Revisited*. Milwaukee, WI: Marquette University Press, 1954.

Vermigli, Peter Martyr. *Philosophical Works: On the Relation of Philosophy to Theology*. Translated and edited by Joseph C. McLelland. Kirksville, MO: Sixteenth Century Essays & Studies, 1996.

Walton, John. *The Lost World of Genesis One: Ancient Cosmology and the Origins Debate*. Downers Grove, IL: InterVarsity Press, 2009.

Whiston, William, trans. *The Works of Josephus: Complete and Unabridged*. Peabody: Hendrickson, 1987.

Witherington, Ben, III and Darlene Hyatt. *Paul's Letter to the Romans: A Socio-Rhetorical Commentary*. Grand Rapids: Wm. B. Eerdmans Publishing, 2004.

Wippel, John F. *The Metaphysical Thought of Thomas Aquinas: From Finite Being to Uncreated Being*. Washington, D. C.: Catholic University of America Press, 2000.

Wright, N. T. "The Letter to the Romans." In *The New Interpreter's Bible, Vol. 10: Acts, Romans, 1 Corinthians*, edited by Leander E. Keck, 393-770. Nashville, TN: Abingdon Press, 2002.

Yonge, Charles Duke, trans. *The Works of Philo: Complete and Unabridged*. Peabody, MA: Hendrickson, 1995.

Young, Edward J. *The Book of Isaiah*. 1972; repr., Grand Rapids: Wm. B. Eerdmans Publishing, 1979.

Zanchi, Girolamo. *On the Law in General*. Translated and edited by Jeffrey J. Veenstra. Sources in Early Modern Economics, Ethics, and Law. Grand Rapids: Christian's Library Press, 2012.

ABOUT THE DAVENANT INSTITUTE

The Davenant Institute supports the renewal of Christian wisdom for the contemporary church. It seeks to sponsor historical scholarship at the intersection of the church and academy, build networks of friendship and collaboration within the Reformed and evangelical world, and equip the saints with time-tested resources for faithful public witness.

We are a nonprofit organization supported by your tax-deductible gifts. Learn more about us, and donate, at www.davenantinstitute.org.

Made in the USA
Columbia, SC
11 August 2023

21456011R10078